Great Commission Soul Winning & Discipleship

By

Steve West

www.xulonpress.com

To Rhoda Ann
a Co-worker at JAISO
during the 1940's with
Velma & me —
            Jewel Sundbeck
                2014

ACKNOWLEDGEMENTS

*T*his book is first dedicated to the Lord for giving me the inspiration. It is also dedicated to all who may come into the Kingdom of God and benefit from its pages. However, there is that exceptional person who formed my early years around knowing and serving the Lord. That person would be my late paternal grandmother. She was, without question, the godliest woman I have ever known. She tirelessly served others before herself. Time and time again she would be cooking, cleaning, or ministering to someone in some way. She was Christianity in action, to say the least. I remember her holding her worn Bible, and the way that she would smile when she talked about Jesus. She always made sure that I knew just how much the Lord loved me. My grandmother was the Christian inspiration and role model who made a difference in my life. Furthermore, special thanks to my sweet wife (Lucy) who encouraged and motivated me during this entire process.

TABLE OF CONTENTS

INTRODUCTION

*H*ave you ever gone into a tire store and noticed all of the various tire types and sizes? Although the wheel was invented thousands of years ago, man has not stopped improving on that simple concept. There are wheels and tires for everything from roller skates to massive, earth-moving construction equipment. Your vehicle probably has just the right wheels and tires for it to roll properly. This book is similar to the tires in a tire store; it is not a new concept. However, it will hopefully be just the right fit for people who are trying to understand the Christian faith. It is designed to be a short lesson, group study workbook about basic evangelism and discipleship. However, individuals will also gain a wealth of knowledge working independently. There are questions at the end of each chapter designed to challenge the reader. These questions should be discussed and answered in a group setting when possible. I purposely did not include an answer key. This is because I want the reader to learn to search and find without being spoon-fed all the answers. The more mature Christians in a group should help guide the less mature in the faith through the process. **When the reader has completed this book, they should have a working knowledge of how to fulfill any part of the Great Commission, and be able to teach others how**

to do the same. As you study the pages of this book, you should have your Bible and a notebook with you. You will need your Bible to look up various scripture references throughout this book. Do not forget to check out "Appendix A" and "Appendix B" found in the back of this book. There you will find valuable resources which will help you on your mission. Feel free to use "Appendix A" as a gospel tract. Furthermore, I have used four different versions of Scripture throughout this book; the KJV, NKJV, NASU, and the NIV from PC Study Bible V4. I have added *italics* to most of the Scriptures referenced herein. May God be with you, and bless you abundantly, as you begin this life-changing study.

CHAPTER ONE

The Power of a Shared Testimony

❋

*D*oris seemed a bit apprehensive about going with her friend, Susan, to a luncheon. Susan reassured Doris that it was only for two hours, and the food was free of charge. The two ladies sat near the front with their plates loaded with food. After a few minutes, a young man stepped up to the microphone and introduced himself as Sam. He began to tell a few clean jokes and funny stories. Doris seemed to lighten up a bit as she laughed along with everyone else.

After about ten minutes of relaxing the crowd with his humor, Sam began to tell how his life had not always been fun and games. Sam told about his childhood with alcoholic parents. He told about his own bout with drugs and alcohol addiction. Finally, after a long period of losing job after job because of his lifestyle, he found himself at the end of his own short rope. Sam took his last bit of money and checked into a cheap motel for the night. Sam's dad had left him only one thing when he passed away; his pistol. This was the night that Sam was going to leave his pain behind and check out of this life.

Sam recalled how he wanted to get the full benefit from his motel room before he did what he came to do. He was going to order a pizza, take a long hot bath, and watch television. Sam noticed that he did not have any drugs or alcohol with him that night. There was no money left to buy anything. He thought about robbing the liquor store down the street. After all, what could they do to him? By the time that they found him, it would be too late.

As Sam reached over to turn off the television, a man was speaking about his past. He spoke about his life in such a way that Sam could relate to everything that the man described. The man went on to tell how he had cried out to God for help. God not only heard his cry for help, but had saved him from certain death and eternal punishment. Sam described to his audience how he just sat there, helpless to move, as he listened to the man tell his story. The man on the television said that God had given him a new life through Jesus Christ. God had taken away all the pain and suffering that he had grown up enduring. This man also offered the same hope and healing to anyone who wanted to be set free. Sam could feel a lump in his throat. Could it honestly be that easy? If there is a God, why would He give a flip about me? This was all a bit overwhelming for Sam, considering the lifestyle that he had been living.

The man went on to explain that it does not matter who you are, or what you have done in your life, Jesus will save you if you ask Him for salvation. The man then offered to lead a prayer for anyone who wanted a second chance at life; real life. Sam fell to his knees and bowed his head. He repeated a prayer with the man on the television, and asked Jesus to save him. Sam explained how he was immediately set free from the thoughts of suicide. He sat on the edge of the bed crying tears of joy and relief. Sam was literally being set free from years of pinned up anger, addiction, and shame at that moment.

Sam realized that he had been changed from within. He also realized that he had to get rid of the pistol that he had with him. He decided to sell it at the local pawn shop. As he hurried out the door, he bumped into a man who was out walking and praying. The man noticed that Sam had been crying and asked him if he was okay. This friendly man introduced himself as a pastor from a nearby church. Sam could not believe what he was hearing. He immediately shared with the pastor what had just taken place. After the pastor had talked with Sam awhile, he made arrangements with one of the church families for Sam to have a short-term place to stay. As Sam concluded his story, he offered the same opportunity for his audience to receive Christ as he had done several years ago. Many people received Jesus as Lord and Savior that night.

Doris decided that she would wait. She had not come from a life of drugs and alcohol. In fact, she had just the opposite experience in life. Doris came from a very wealthy, affluent family. She had the best education that money could buy. She had never gone without and was quite content with her life and career. She only went to the luncheon to appease her friend, Susan. On the way home, Susan asked Doris what she thought about Sam's testimony. Doris explained that she couldn't really relate to what Sam had gone through, but she was glad that religion had helped him. Doris went on to say that just because it worked for Sam does not mean that it works for everybody. Doris told Susan about her wonderful job, home, and family. She just didn't have time for a "crutch" like religion. Besides, she was up for promotion to office manager soon. Everything seemed to be going her way.

Susan prayed silently. She then asked Doris if she believed that there was a God. Doris replied that she believes in God, but never actually needed anything from Him. She was living large without anyone's help. Susan began to explain how the Pharisees were of important status and lovers of money in their day. Then Susan quoted what Jesus had to say to them:

Luke 16:14-15

14 Now the Pharisees, who were lovers of money, also heard all these things, and they derided Him. 15 And He [Jesus] said to them, "You are those who justify yourselves before men, but God knows your hearts. For what is highly esteemed among men is an abomination in the sight of God." NKJV

Susan boldly shared with her friend: "Doris, you may have done all the right things in the sight of man. However, Jesus said that a person must be born again to see the Kingdom of God. It would be a shame if you gained the whole world and then lost your soul, Doris." As they pulled into the driveway, Doris thanked Susan for the invite and went into her house.

Her husband was away on business, and the children were staying the night at grandma's house. Later that evening, the events of the day replayed in her mind. Doris began to tear up and then to sob uncontrollably. No one had ever said these things to her before. She had always been a strong person in control of her own life.

Doris began to call out to God. She asked Him to save her as He had done for Sam, and her friend Susan. She felt an instant peace fill the room and soon fell asleep. When Doris awoke, she immediately called her friend Susan to tell her what had happened. The two rejoiced over coffee and pancakes. Doris began studying the Word of God with a passion she never had before.

It has been six years since Doris received Jesus as Lord of her life. Since then, her children and husband have also become followers of Jesus. Doris and her husband, Brian, recently graduated Bible College and have become missionaries. Doris shares her testimony at every opportunity that presents itself. She is forever grateful to her friend, Susan, who spoke the truth to her when nobody else dared.

Closing Thoughts:

Every saved person has a testimony of how they came to know Jesus Christ as Lord and Savior of their life. Just going to church, or knowing that there is a God, does not make a person saved. You should know and remember that moment when you surrendered your own life to Christ. This is your unique story that Satan cannot take away. However, he will make you think that your story is insignificant in relation to someone else's testimony. Your story may be the very thing that helps someone find Christ today. Remember this one thing: **The only testimony that God cannot use is the testimony that is not shared!**

Things to Consider:

1. Why had Doris attended the luncheon?

2. How many people can you list that had a role in helping Sam find Christ? (Both directly and indirectly)

3. What did Susan do before telling Doris what she needed to hear?

4. Although Doris couldn't relate to Sam's testimony, what and/or who made Doris realize that she needed a Savior?

5. Read Ephesians 2:10. What "works" or fruit came from Doris when she got saved?

6. How did you come to know Jesus as Lord of your life? If you do not yet have a personal testimony of how you came to know Jesus Christ as Lord and Savior of your life, then Chapter Two is especially for you.

CHAPTER TWO

Do You Have Something to Share?

*I*t is impossible to share with others what you do not possess. Just believing that there is a God is not enough to save you from eternal wrath and condemnation. In fact, it puts you on the same level as the demons, according to Scripture:

James 2:19
You believe that there is one God. You do well. Even the demons believe—and tremble! NKJV

So what is it that will set you apart from the demons? See what Jesus had to say to Nicodemus; a teacher of Israel:

John 3:3-7
3 Jesus answered and said to him, "Most assuredly, I say to you, unless one is born again, he cannot see the kingdom of God."

4 Nicodemus said to Him, "How can a man be born when he is old? Can he enter a second time into his mother's womb and be born?"

5 Jesus answered, "Most assuredly, I say to you, unless one is born of water and the Spirit, he cannot enter the kingdom of God. 6 That which is born of the flesh is flesh, and that which is born of the Spirit is spirit. 7 Do not marvel that I said to you, 'You must be born again." NKJV

Your professional or financial status in this world will not help you enter the Kingdom of God. Nicodemus learned this by his conversation with Jesus. Flesh gives birth to flesh; this is our natural birth. However, new spiritual birth can only come from God because Spirit gives birth to spirit. In fact, "born again" as referenced in the Greek, means "born from above." Here are just three results of being born again by the Spirit of God:

Romans 8:1
There is therefore now no condemnation to those who are in Christ Jesus, who do not walk according to the flesh, but according to the Spirit. NKJV

2 Corinthians 5:17
Therefore, if anyone is in Christ, he is a new creation; old things have passed away; behold, all things have become new. NKJV

1 John 5:12
He who has the Son has life; he who does not have the Son of God does not have life. NKJV

Sadly, there are many people who believe that they are on their way to Heaven because they: 1) Grew up in church; 2) Their parents are Christians; 3) They are faithful to make a church service on Easter and Christmas, etc. Many people who attend church regularly are not saved. I grew up in a certain mainline denomination and never understood what being "born again" meant. Years later, when I was a young man in my 20s, someone took the time to share the gospel message with me at a diner. I believed in God, but I was still dead in my sins.

So how can a person actually become born again by the Spirit of God? They must first understand that there is only ONE way to be saved, and that is through Jesus Christ. Why? Because this was the plan of God who created all things, including all humans. If there were many paths that lead to God, then Jesus is a liar. After all, Jesus did say that He was the only way to the Father. He also said that a person cannot inherit the Kingdom of God unless they are born again. See for yourself:

John 14:6
Jesus said to him, "I am the way, the truth, and the life. No one comes to the Father except through Me." NKJV

Acts 4:10-12
10 ". . . let it be known to you all, and to all the people of Israel, that by the name of Jesus Christ of Nazareth, whom you crucified, whom God raised from the dead, by Him this man stands here before you whole. 11 This is the 'stone which was rejected by you builders, which has become the chief cornerstone.' 12 Nor is there salvation in any other, for there is no other name under Heaven given among men by which we must be saved." NKJV

It would not make sense for God to send His only begotten Son to suffer and die a horrible death on a cross for our sins if there were other ways to be saved. Remember this: Satan does not want people to be saved. Therefore, he will put up many stumbling blocks (including false religions) to keep people from finding THE Truth in Jesus Christ.

If you have not yet done so, now is the time to be reconciled to God. You can become born again by the Holy Spirit of the one true, living God. You can start living the life that you were created to live. Here are a few verses that will help guide you through the process of salvation.

Acts 17:30-31
30 "Truly, these times of ignorance God overlooked, but now commands all men everywhere to repent, 31 because He has appointed a day on which He will judge the world in righteousness by the Man whom He has ordained. He has given assurance of this to all by raising Him from the dead." NKJV

Acts 3:19
Repent therefore and be converted, that your sins may be blotted out, so that times of refreshing may come from the presence of the Lord, . . . NKJV

1 John 1:9
If we confess our sins, He is faithful and just to forgive us our sins and to cleanse us from all unrighteousness. NKJV

Repent simply means to turn around and go the other way. The picture that I get in my mind is that we are all born sinners facing Satan with our back toward God. When we have repented, or turned around, we are then facing God with our back toward Satan. We are then heading away from the one who wants to destroy us, and heading toward the One who wants to save us. So what comes after repentance?

Romans 10:9-13

9 ". . . that if you confess with your mouth the Lord Jesus and believe in your heart that God has raised Him from the dead, you will be saved. 10 For with the heart one believes unto righteousness, and with the mouth confession is made unto salvation. 11 For the Scripture says, "Whoever believes on Him will not be put to shame. 12 For there is no distinction between Jew and Greek, for the same Lord over all is rich to all who call upon Him. 13 For whoever calls on the name of the LORD shall be saved." NKJV

To simplify what we have just covered, we must: Confess and repent of our sins; confess with our mouth and believe in our heart that Jesus Christ is Lord; and believe that God raised Him up from the dead on the third day. **"Whoever calls on the name of the Lord will be saved."** What a great promise from God. Why wait or put off free eternal life?

John 3:18

He who believes in Him is not condemned; but he who does not believe is condemned already, because he has not believed in the name of the only begotten Son of God. NKJV

Here is a sample prayer that can be prayed when asking the Lord Jesus into your life:

Lord, I acknowledge and confess my sins before You. I have sinned against You, and I now repent of my sins which have separated me from You. I believe that Jesus suffered and died in my place on the cross. I believe that He arose from the dead on the third day according to

the Holy Scriptures. I now place my faith and trust in Jesus Christ for my salvation. Come into my life and fill me with Your Holy Spirit. Thank You for saving me, Lord. Amen.

John 1:12-13

12 But as many as received Him, to them He gave the right to become children of God, to those who believe in His name: 13 who were born, not of blood, nor of the will of the flesh, nor of the will of man, but of God. NKJV

If you did pray to receive Christ as your personal Savior, your name is now written in the Lamb's Book of Life. You have passed from eternal death and punishment to eternal life and blessings. Best of all, you are now a new creature in Christ! The God of the universe has become your Father! So what now? Seek fellowship with other believers in a Christ honoring, Bible teaching church that can disciple you in God's Word. **Be obedient and follow Jesus in baptism.** Whether you were "baptized" as an infant or in early childhood, you should make a new public profession of your new faith in Christ. Full immersion represents the true baptism. It is your public witness of identifying with the death, burial and resurrection of Jesus Christ. Spend time with the Lord daily in prayer and in His Word. Now you can share your new faith with your friends and family. Remember to be patient with them just as God has been patient with you.

Components of a Personal Testimony

Picture yourself on a witness stand in a courtroom. You are about to give an eyewitness account of what you have seen and/or heard in relation to an event that happened. You are bearing witness to the events that you personally experienced. Notice what Jesus told the disciples of John the Baptist when they asked Him if He was the One that was to come:

Luke 7:20-22

20 When the men had come to Him, they said, "John the Baptist has sent us to You, saying, 'Are You the Coming One, or do we look for another?'" 21 And that very hour He cured many of infirmities, afflictions, and evil spirits; and to many blind He gave sight. 22 Jesus answered and said to them, "Go and tell John the things you have seen and heard: that the blind see, the lame walk, the lepers are cleansed, the deaf hear, the dead are raised, the poor have the gospel preached to them." NKJV

Jesus sent them back to "testify" as to what they had seen and heard Jesus doing (Verse 21). One other powerful illustration was when Jesus delivered a man from his many demons. The man wanted to go with Jesus but Jesus responded in this manner:

Luke 8:38-39

38 Now the man from whom the demons had departed begged Him that he might be with Him. But Jesus sent him away, saying, 39 "Return to your own house, and tell what great things God has done for you." And he went his way and proclaimed throughout the whole city what great things Jesus had done for him. NKJV

Both, the disciples of John the Baptist and the man delivered from demons, now have a testimony to share. They can testify of their own personal encounter with the Lord Jesus Christ. Your testimony is the story of *your* personal encounter with the Lord. One HUGE misconception about testimonies is that they have to be an instant, earth-shattering experience that saved you from a life of drugs and alcohol.

However, your testimony should have some key elements that explain your life before and after your salvation experience. A personal encounter with the God of the universe does not leave a person unchanged.

Satan is the only one who will try to convince you that your testimony is not worth sharing. You have no idea what will (or will not) relate to a person at any given time. **Every born again follower of Jesus Christ has a valid story to tell about how they became a child of the living God through Jesus Christ.** Again, the only testimony that God cannot use is the one that is not shared.

YOUR PERSONAL TESTIMONY IS:

Your Story – This is your personal salvation experience with Jesus Christ. It is the story of what God has done in your life. Your changed life in Christ will validate your testimony if lived out by faith, love, obedience, and God's Word. If you have not changed from your old lifestyle, then you do not have a salvation testimony. In fact, you probably had a false conversion experience.

Relational – Humans were all created related from Adam and Eve. Therefore, we are relational beings. When God gave Moses the Ten Commandments, each commandment had to do with either our relationship to God, or our relationship to each other. Our testimony is simply telling others about how our new relationship with God has changed our relationship with everyone else. After all, becoming a "new creature in Christ" changes everything. Jesus empowers us to forgive, restore, and pursue healthy relationships. Once a person is saved, they can now relate to the lost and the saved.

Hope Giving – Your testimony is simply what God has done for you. If you are now living the victorious life in Jesus Christ, people will see that you handle life's situations in a much different way than before. A train tunnel devoid of light in either direction pretty much sums up a person's life without Christ. Each day is more of the same, with no real meaning or purpose to life. Even wealthy people find that their money can only buy stuff and not true happiness. Once the person in the train tunnel sees daylight, there is instant joy. Even though the person is still in the tunnel, there is now a solid hope in their future because of the daylight ahead. It is natural to want to share that good news with others who are lost in the tunnel so that they can also share the joy of having hope. At this time, please read **1 Peter 3:15.**

Non-confrontational – Testimonies are rarely, if ever, confrontational. They are simply the story of what God has done in your life. People cannot argue with the experiences that you have had in your own life. However, your story will still plant, water, or harvest a seed that has already been planted. Even hardcore skeptics are searching for hope and truth. Your story, presented in love, might be the one thing that a person needed to hear without enduring confrontation.

Expiration Free – Your story will never expire because it is just like your physical birthday. You will pass on one day, but your birthday and your testimony will be a legacy left behind for others to remember. Your testimony will still be just as fresh a hundred years from now as it was the day you first believed. Never "outgrow" sharing your testimony with others. It will usually open the spiritual doors to a person's heart.

Closing Thoughts:

Living a transformed life validates your testimony. Action always speaks louder than words. Guard your testimony by guarding your life. Guard your life by the Holy Spirit and the Word of God.

Things to Consider:

1. What validates our testimony better than anything else could in the eyes of others?

2. How can our testimony give hope to someone who might be searching for truth?

3. What is the only testimony that God cannot use?

4. How many years should your personal testimony be used in witnessing?

5. Should I share my testimony with someone who is far above or below my social/economic status? Why or why not?

6. When was the last time that you shared your testimony with an unsaved person? What were the results?

CHAPTER THREE

Introduction to Spiritual Warfare

*S*piritual warfare is a reality. In a nutshell, it is the ongoing battle between God and Satan. Lucifer (a.k.a. Satan) is a created being and was once a mighty Archangel in Heaven. He became jealous of God and, because of pride, wanted to overthrow God and sit upon the throne of the Most High. So, along with one-third of the angels, Lucifer attempted to overthrow God in Heaven by force. After this attempt, Lucifer was cast down to the earth along with the rebelling angels. These rebel angels are now believed to be the demons who are active here on this earth. However, it is not exactly known who demons are, or from where they came. What we do know is that they belong to the kingdom of darkness. This means that all humanity has a 24/7 common enemy; Satan and his demonic realm.

Isaiah 14:12-15
How you are fallen from Heaven, O Lucifer, son of the morning! How you are cut down to the ground, you who weakened the nations! 13 For you have said in your

heart: 'I will ascend into Heaven, I will exalt my throne above the stars of God; I will also sit on the mount of the congregation on the farthest sides of the north; 14 I will ascend above the heights of the clouds, I will be like the Most High.' 15 Yet you shall be brought down to Sheol, to the lowest depths of the Pit. NKJV

Satan continued his rebellion against Eve in the Garden of Eden. This set in motion the results and consequences of the fall of mankind. Please take a moment to read the third chapter of the book of *Genesis* in your Bible at this time. This chapter is extremely important because it is the foundation for: 1) The fall of man; 2) The curse of the earth; 3) The first shedding of blood to cover sins (skins that God gave to Adam and Eve as a covering; 4) the promised Messiah; 5) Satan's eventual downfall through the work of the coming Messiah.

Jesus referred to Satan as a liar and murderer from the beginning. Satan deceives and destroys lives wherever he can. There are numerous incidents of spiritual battles, both in the Old, and the New Testaments. Many times throughout history, spiritual battles have turned into physical battles. Where evil is present, there is darkness and oppression. Where the Spirit of the Lord is present, there is light and liberty. Evil has no authority over God or His people. It is extremely important that you grasp the concept that a Christian can only be "oppressed" by the forces of evil. Christians cannot be "possessed" by an evil spirit.

1 John 4:4
You are of God, little children, and have overcome them, because He who is in you is greater than he who is in the world. NKJV

Since the fall of man through Adam, we are sinners by default. We do not become sinners when we break God's commandments. On the contrary, we break God's commandments because we are *born* into sin. We are helpless in sin without external intervention from God. God offers us much more than salvation alone. He indwells those who have placed their faith and trust in Jesus Christ with His Holy Spirit. It is by God's indwelling Holy Spirit that we have power and dominion over Satan and his demonic forces. These two opposing entities can never coexist together within the same body.

Not only are Christians "overcomers" of the evil one, the Holy Spirit also discerns truth from error for God's people. Most battles, whether spiritual or physical, begin in the mind. Our "world views" "are shaped according to what we believe spiritually. Remember, there are ultimately only two world views, spiritually speaking. A person's world view is either guided by the spirit of the air and prince of this world's systems; or, by the Spirit of God. There is no middle ground.

People naturally seek to gratify their flesh and sinful nature. The verses below explain how this works:

Romans 8:5-9
5 For those who live according to the flesh set their minds on the things of the flesh, but those who live according to the Spirit, the things of the Spirit. 6 For to be carnally minded is death, but to be spiritually minded is life and peace. 7 Because the carnal mind is enmity against God; for it is not subject to the law of God, nor indeed can be. 8 So then, those who are in the flesh cannot please God. 9 But you are not in the flesh but in the Spirit, if indeed the Spirit of God dwells in you. Now if anyone does not have the Spirit of Christ, he is not His. NKJV

These verses capture the very essence of spiritual warfare. Remember, we were created in the image of God. That alone makes us a target for Satan. It does not matter if a person believes in God, angels, demons, Satan, or any part of the supernatural. You are NOT exempt from spiritual attacks from Satan and the forces of evil. There is no social status on earth that is safe from spiritual attacks by the forces of evil. However, the good news is that there is also no social status on earth that God's love and offer of salvation can't reach.

Many people who are not saved are deceived into thinking that all is well. They believe that spiritual things are a waste of time. Other people could not imagine living one more day without some kind of hope apart from their current situation. However, once a person is born again by the Spirit of the living God, their spiritual eyes are opened to spiritual things, and they see clearly what they could not see before. This is why Jesus said: *"And you shall know the truth, and the truth shall make you free." John 8:32 NKJV*

Of course, the opposite of truth is a lie, and lies are meant to deceive. So Jesus sets us free from the bondage of deception by Satan. Understanding these truths about spiritual warfare helps us to see the big picture. See what Jesus said about Himself:

John 14:6
Jesus said to him, "I am the way, the truth, and the life. No one comes to the Father except through Me." NKJV

Since Jesus is THE Way, THE Truth, and THE Life, the exact opposite is true for Satan. He is NOT the way because he has NO truth in him, and he TAKES life from people. Satan schemes and deceives only to keep people away from the knowledge of God and His plan for salvation through Jesus Christ. But thanks to the indwelling Holy Spirit inside all believers, we are not (and should not) be ignorant of his schemes:

2 Corinthians 2:11

11. . . lest Satan should take advantage of us; for we are not ignorant of his devices. NKJV

God has also provided a way to stand against the schemes and devices of Satan:

Ephesians 6:11-13

11 Put on the whole armor of God, that you may be able to stand against the wiles of the devil. 12 For we do not wrestle against flesh and blood, but against principalities, against powers, against the rulers of the darkness of this age, against spiritual hosts of wickedness in the heavenly places. NKJV

We will cover more about God's armor later. Just understand that God has provided everything that we need to effectively combat the forces of evil.

I want you to read the following verses and see the world view change that happens when we receive Christ. Being born-again actually does make us a new creation in Christ. Along with our new world view and identity comes a new title and mission. A rescue mission:

2 Corinthians 5:16-21

16 So from now on we regard no one from a worldly point of view. Though we once regarded Christ in this way, we do so no longer. 17 Therefore, if anyone is in Christ, he is a new creation; the old has gone, the new has come! 18 All this is from God, who reconciled us to himself through Christ and gave us the ministry of reconciliation: 19 that God was reconciling the world to himself in Christ, not counting men's sins against them. And he has committed to us the message of reconciliation. 20 We are therefore Christ's ambassadors, as though God were making his appeal through us. We implore you on Christ's behalf: Be reconciled to God. 21 God made him who had no sin to be sin for us, so that in him we might become the righteousness of God. NIV

Now that we have been set free, our mission as ambassadors for Christ is to tell others about what God has done for us. Jesus gives us spiritual authority to accomplish His missions. Remember the seventy that Jesus sent out to preach the Good News? They had spiritual authority over demonic forces:

Luke 10:17-20
17 Then the seventy returned with joy, saying, "Lord, even the demons are subject to us in Your name." 18 And He said to them, "I saw Satan fall like lightning from Heaven. 19 Behold, I give you the authority to trample on serpents and scorpions, and over all the power of the enemy, and nothing shall by any means hurt you. 20 Nevertheless, do not rejoice in this, that the spirits are subject to you, but rather rejoice because your names are written in Heaven." NKJV

Satan only has the power that God allows him to have over any circumstance. In the O.T. Book of Job, Satan asked God if he could have his way with Job to get him to curse God and die. God allowed Satan to do whatever he wished to Job except take his life. What we must understand about God is that He will not lose to Satan. Not only did Job recover from his illness; he was restored with much more than he had when Satan began his experiment with Job. The story of Job has since motivated and inspired many people who have faced various trials and hardships. What Satan thought was a sure thing ultimately backfired in his face. Rest in the fact the God is sovereign above ALL.

Closing Thoughts:

Those without Christ do not and cannot fully understand that they are deceived by Satan. They have no understanding of spiritual things according to the Word of God. It is only after our eyes have been opened to spiritual truth by the Holy Spirit that we are enabled to understand spiritual concepts such as spiritual warfare. It is absolutely crucial for believers to understand their role in spiritual warfare.

2 Cor 4:3-5
3 And even if our gospel is veiled, it is veiled to those who are perishing, 4 in whose case the god of this world has blinded the minds of the unbelieving so that they might not see the light of the gospel of the glory of Christ, who is the image of God. NASU

Things to Consider:

1. What was Lucifer's downfall?

2. Is it possible to be spiritually neutral in life? Why or why not?

3. Are there still spiritual battles going on today? Why?

4. Who indwells all Christians that the unsaved do not possess?

5. What authority does Satan have over God and/or His people?

The Nuts and Bolts of Spiritual Warfare

At any given point in time, there are many battles being fought in the spiritual or "supernatural" realm. God's angels are fighting for God and His Kingdom, which include His people while they are on this earth. When God's people pray, supernatural things occur. Believers have a spiritual arsenal of heavenly hosts ready to fight on our behalf. Read the following familiar verses again to understand more about this concept:

2 Corinthians 10:3-6
3 For though we walk in the flesh, we do not war according to the flesh. 4 For the weapons of our warfare are not carnal but mighty in God for pulling down strongholds, 5 casting down arguments and every high thing that exalts itself against the knowledge of God, bringing every thought into captivity to the obedience of Christ, 6 and being ready to punish all disobedience when your obedience is fulfilled. NKJV

Psalms 34:7
The angel of the LORD encamps all around those who fear Him, and delivers them. NKJV

Every Christian should also be well versed regarding the armor and battlefields of Spiritual Warfare. You cannot prepare enough to stand against the waves of evil coming from the demonic realm.

Ephesians 6:10-20

10 Finally, my brethren, be strong in the Lord and in the power of His might. 11 Put on the whole armor of God, that you may be able to stand against the wiles of the devil. 12 For we do not wrestle against flesh and blood, but against principalities, against powers, against the rulers of the darkness of this age, against spiritual hosts of wickedness in the heavenly places. 13 Therefore take up the whole armor of God, that you may be able to withstand in the evil day, and having done all, to stand. 14 Stand therefore, having girded your waist with truth, having put on the breastplate of righteousness, 15 and having shod your feet with the preparation of the gospel of peace; 16 above all, taking the shield of faith with which you will be able to quench all the fiery darts of the wicked one. 17 And take the helmet of salvation, and the sword of the Spirit, which is the word of God; 18 praying always with all prayer and supplication in the Spirit, being watchful to this end with all perseverance and supplication for all the saints 19 and for me, that utterance may be given to me, that I may open my mouth boldly to make known the mystery of the gospel, 20 for which I am an ambassador in chains; that in it I may speak boldly, as I ought to speak. NKJV

While Satan has no authority over any of God's children, he can hinder our work and our lives with various obstacles. However, our Heavenly Father has given us a full arsenal, complete with spiritual body armor, to stand firm against the wiles (or schemes) of the Devil. Our failure to use our arsenal causes us to stall or backslide spiritually.

The main components of the armor include: truth, righteousness, being prepared with the gospel, faith, salvation, and our sword, which is the Word of God. Combined with prayer, the enemy doesn't stand a chance. Let's look at one key "battlefield" of spiritual warfare:

The Mind:

Romans 12:2
And do not be conformed to this world, but be transformed by the renewing of your mind, that you may prove what is that good and acceptable and perfect will of God. NKJV

As part of being a "new creature in Christ" (**2 Cor. 5:17**), we also renew our minds from the futile thinking of the world. The Holy Spirit gives us the "mind of Christ" according to **1 Cor. 2:16** and **Phil. 2:5-8.** This part of our body is covered by the "helmet of salvation." Without salvation, we would not have the mind of Christ. This allows all believers to be like minded in purpose and Spirit.

There is an ongoing battle for the mind. Satan knows that if he can distract you long enough, he can tempt and/or deceive you into doing things that will discredit your testimony and render you ineffective for the Kingdom of God. Notice what James says:

James 1:14-15
14 But each one is tempted when he is drawn away by his own desires and enticed. 15 Then, when desire has conceived, it gives birth to sin; and sin, when it is full-grown, brings forth death. NKJV

The death of humanity is Satan's ultimate goal. Just look at the number of people today who are caught up in sins that can, and will eventually lead to death. All of these addictions and entrapments were first considered in the mind of the person before becoming an action by the person. Scripture continually warns us to guard our hearts and our minds for this reason. We choose to give into sin; we don't have to give into it. Giving into sin is always a choice. God makes away for us to avoid sin if we so choose.

1 Corinthians 10:13
No temptation has overtaken you except such as is common to man; but God is faithful, who will not allow you to be tempted beyond what you are able, but with the temptation will also make the way of escape, that you may be able to bear it. NKJV

Philippians 4:8
Finally, brethren, whatever things are true, whatever things are noble, whatever things are just, whatever things are pure, whatever things are lovely, whatever things are of good report, if there is any virtue and if there is anything praiseworthy—meditate on these things. NKJV

If we continually renew our mind with the Word of God, then we will be prepared and equipped to cast away temptation, fear, and doubt when the enemy attacks. There are several key components of society where Satan likes to attack and control. So far, you have just looked at the importance of guarding your mind. But where else should we expect spiritual battles to occur. How about anywhere there are people. Politics, education, families (as ordained by God in His Word), television, radio, churches, the mission field, and social clubs are all battlefields. These are places where the two main world views (Satan's agenda vs. God's plan) will always be at war with each other. It doesn't take a rocket scientist to see what is happening on the evening news. All the corruption, shootings, drugs, etc., were not God's plans on how things should work. Satan deceived people into thinking that they somehow know better than God about how to run their lives. If more Christians would stand their ground, the forces of evil wouldn't be gaining as much ground as they have in recent years.

Preparing for Action:

Understanding the times is a must. You don't have to be a Bible scholar to understand that we are at least in the beginning stages of the end times. It is imperative that Christians put on the whole armor of God if we are going to make a difference. As a Christian, anywhere in this world should be considered "behind enemy lines." God tells us to put on His full armor. I have never seen a verse that tells us to take off any part of His armor. Only Satan would like to see you out of God's armor and vulnerable.

1 Peter 1:13-16
13 Therefore, prepare your minds for action; be self-controlled; set your hope fully on the grace to be given you when Jesus Christ is revealed. 14 As obedient children, do not conform to the evil desires you had when you lived in ignorance. 15 But just as he who called you is holy, so be holy in all you do; 16 for it is written: "Be holy, because I am holy." NIV

As you can see by the verses above, part of being prepared is living a holy life. Living a holy life is a life that glorifies the Lord. Glorifying our Heavenly Father with our lives should be every Christian's desire.

Colossians 3:17
And whatever you do in word or deed, do all in the name of the Lord Jesus, giving thanks to God the Father through Him. NKJV

1 Corinthians 10:31
31 Therefore, whether you eat or drink, or whatever you do, do all to the glory of God. NKJV

So to effectively stand our ground in spiritual warfare, we must guard our hearts and minds against satanic or demonic schemes. We must also put on the whole armor of God, and live holy lives that glorify God. Cast out all fear and doubt which gives the enemy a foothold. God's Word reminds us several times not to fear, worry, or doubt but have faith.

A key part of guarding and preparing one's self for any spiritual battle is prayer. Obviously, there are personal prayers where you are taking care of personal matters. But there are also intercessory prayers. Intercessory prayers are prayers that intercede on the behalf of others. This key component in the believer's arsenal will usually mean the difference between victory or defeat. The Apostle Paul's personal prayers were usually asking God to help him to be bold in sharing the gospel. However, Paul was always interceding on behalf of the saints.

Prayer, fasting, and the Word of God are extremely important in the breaking down of spiritual strongholds. There are nations, tribes, cities, and various people groups that have demonic strongholds over their entire region. Some of these strongholds require months or years of prayer and fasting to demolish. One recent example of such a place is the Republic of Haiti. For years, missionaries had prayed that a door would open in that country for the gospel of Jesus Christ to enter. Then a major earthquake happened and opened the door for the gospel in a way never seen before in

Haiti. Demonic strongholds were broken, and many Haitians were delivered from years of spiritual bondage when they received Jesus as Lord and Savior of their lives. Evangelism IS spiritual warfare. When you are rescuing people from the grip of Satan, he will put up a fight. The true Christian's attitude should always be: *How many souls can I rescue from the Kingdom of Darkness and bring into the Kingdom of Light?* Of course, Satan wants you to be a bench warmer and stay out of his way. That is why it is not considered "politically correct" to share the gospel in a lost world. Remember to pray for others as much, if not more, than yourself.

Closing Thoughts:

As we move closer to the return of our Lord Jesus Christ, we will be facing more of the things that were prophesied for the end times. Some of these things include an increase in lawlessness; disrespectful children; people not willing to put up with sound doctrine; people who are offended by the name of Jesus; doctrines of demons; etc. Much of this has even infiltrated many churches. Put on, and get used to, the whole armor of God. Satan will try his best to make you ineffective for the Kingdom of God. Bad stewardship of time, finances, marriage, etc., can render many Christians ineffective and/or lukewarm. Remember to always be vigilant. Guard your mind and stay prepared by living holy and praying constantly. Lead others out of the darkness and into the Kingdom of Light by example. Before Joshua went into the Promise Land with the Israelites, the Lord said this to him:

Joshua 1:6-9
6 "Be strong and courageous, because you will lead these people to inherit the land I swore to their forefathers to give them. 7 Be strong and very courageous. Be careful to obey all the law my servant Moses gave you;

do not turn from it to the right or to the left, that you may be successful wherever you go. 8 Do not let this Book of the Law depart from your mouth; meditate on it day and night, so that you may be careful to do everything written in it. Then you will be prosperous and successful. 9 Have I not commanded you? Be strong and courageous. Do not be terrified; do not be discouraged, for the LORD your God will be with you wherever you go." NIV

God has also promised all believers that He will never leave us or forsake us; that the gates of Hell will NOT prevail against His church; no weapon formed against us shall prosper; and that our God is a mighty fortress by which we can take refuge. Be strong and courageous. Demonic forces are setting up many strongholds which keep people from the knowledge of God. Never forget the power found in the blood and name of Jesus. Whether you are praying for someone to be delivered from demonic possession, or simply praying for strongholds to be broken, you will need to proclaim the blood and name of Jesus over the demonic strongholds in question. All authority belongs to Jesus Christ, and he gives his children free access to His authority.

Things to Consider:

1. Why is it important to guard our mind?

2. Name at least four major spiritual battlefields.

3. What does a spiritually prepared Christian life look like?

4. What is the importance of prayer and fasting for the Christian?

5. Why should Christians pray and intercede on the behalf of others?

6. Why would evangelism be spiritual warfare?

CHAPTER FOUR

<u>Knowing</u> the Word of God

*E*very new believer in Jesus Christ, regardless of age, is a spiritual newborn. This term is in no way meant to be condescending. On the contrary, it marks the beginning of an exciting journey in the family of God. Even the original twelve disciples of Jesus went through a spiritual growth process before they set out to fulfill their missions. Just as babies are totally dependent on their parents and other family members, spiritual newborns are dependent on their Heavenly Father, His Word, and their brothers and sisters in the faith. The Bible even says that we begin our spiritual journey as newborns on the milk of the Word of God. *1 Peter 2:2 As newborn babes, desire the sincere milk of the word, that ye may grow thereby: KJV*

In this chapter, we will look at the first of six stages of your personal spiritual growth. The six stages are **KLS-WES,** which stands for **Know, Live, Share-Win, Equip, Send.** All Christians should find themselves somewhere in this KLS-WES scenario as they seek to grow in their faith. A Christian's spiritual growth can be marked by how well they are embracing each of these six steps in their daily walk. The first step is ***"Knowledge."*** After salvation, our spiritual journey should begin by *knowing* what our Heavenly Father has communicated to us in His Word, the Bible. The Bible and the indwelling Holy Spirit combine to give us all that we need to live and grow spiritually. In fact, what you know or don't know can be a matter of life and death. God wants us to know Him and His Word.

Hosea 4:6
My people are destroyed for lack of knowledge. NKJV

2 Peter 1:2-11
*2 Grace and peace be yours in abundance through the **knowledge** of God and of Jesus our Lord. 3 His divine power has given us everything we need for life and godliness through our **knowledge** of him who called us by his own glory and goodness. 4 Through these he has given us his very great and precious promises, so that through them you may participate in the divine nature and escape the corruption in the world caused by evil desires. 5 For this very reason, make every effort to add to your faith goodness; and to goodness, **knowledge**; 6 and to **knowledge**, self-control; and to self-control, perseverance; and to perseverance, godliness; 7 and to godliness, brotherly kindness; and to brotherly kindness, love. 8 For if you possess these qualities in increasing measure, they will keep you from being ineffective and unproductive in your **knowledge** of our Lord Jesus Christ. 9 But if anyone does not have them, he is nearsighted and blind, and has forgotten that he has been cleansed from his past sins. 10 Therefore, my brothers, be all the more eager to make your calling and election sure. For if you do these things, you will never fall, 11 and you will receive a rich welcome into the eternal kingdom of our Lord and Savior Jesus Christ. NIV*

We can clearly see from these verses that knowledge of God and His Word is crucial in regard to personal spiritual growth. In verse two, we have grace and peace in abundance through our knowledge of God and Jesus Christ. In verse three, God has given us everything that we need for life and godliness through our knowledge of Him. In fact, knowledge is only one of seven qualities of our faith mentioned above that we need an ever increasing supply of so that we do not become ineffective and unproductive in our knowledge of our Lord Jesus Christ.

We must understand that when we read the Bible, we are reading the actual Word of God. The Bible is actually 66 books written over a period of 1600 years by 40 different writers, but only one Author, God. Inspired by the Holy Spirit, men would write or speak the Words of God as they were led to do so:

2 Timothy 3:16-17
16 All Scripture is given by inspiration of God, and is profitable for doctrine, for reproof, for correction, for instruction in righteousness, 17 that the man of God may be complete, thoroughly equipped for every good work. NKJV

2 Peter 1:20-21
20 knowing this first, that no prophecy of Scripture is of any private interpretation, 21 for prophecy never came by the will of man, but holy men of God spoke as they were moved by the Holy Spirit. 21 for prophecy never came by the will of man, but holy men of God spoke as they were moved by the Holy Spirit. NKJV

King David had a special place where he treasured God's Word:

Psalms 119:11
Your word I have hidden in my heart, that I might not sin against You. NKJV

Notice why King David kept God's Word in his heart; so that he would not sin against God. We have to know what God expects from us if we are going to live a life that glorifies Him. One thing that you must understand about God's Word is that it is **living** and **active**:

Hebrews 4:12
12 For the word of God is living and active and sharper than any two-edged sword, and piercing as far as the division of soul and spirit, of both joints and marrow, and able to judge the thoughts and intentions of the heart. NASU

The more familiar we become with the Word, the more we can apply it to all aspects of our daily lives. His Word speaks to us where we are spiritually at any given time. In fact, the Holy Spirit knows what you need before you do. But understand this; our common enemy, Satan, will stop at nothing to keep you from gaining the knowledge of God which leads to understanding and life.

The enemy knows that the more truth that you know and understand, the more you will also know and understand lies, deception, and their source. Note the following verses:

Proverbs 9:10-11
10 "The fear of the LORD is the beginning of wisdom, And the knowledge of the Holy One is understanding. 11 For by me your days will be multiplied, And years of life will be added to you. NKJV

Knowledge can be abused and cause pride to swell up in a person. However, the more that we learn about God, the more humble it should make us. It is like an ant that finds a grain of sugar and thinks that it now knows and understands everything pertaining to agriculture based on one grain of sugar. Being a good steward of our knowledge of God's Word means that we live out what we learn in a way that glorifies God. It is only by the grace of God that you understand what you now know.

John 16:13-15
13 However, when He, the Spirit of truth, has come, He will guide you into all truth; for He will not speak on His own authority, but whatever He hears He will speak; and He will tell you things to come. 14 He will glorify Me, for He will take of what is Mine and declare it to you. 15 All things that the Father has are Mine. Therefore I said that He will take of Mine and declare it to you. NKJV

1 Corinthians 2:10-16
10 but God has revealed it to us by his Spirit. The Spirit searches all things, even the deep things of God. 11 For who among men knows the thoughts of a man except the man's spirit within him? In the same way no one knows the thoughts of God except the Spirit of God. 12 We have not received the spirit of the world but the Spirit who is from God, that we may understand what God has freely given us. 13 This is what we speak, not in words taught us by human wisdom but in words taught by the Spirit, expressing spiritual truths in spiritual words. 14 The man without the Spirit does not accept the things that come from the Spirit of God, for they are foolishness to him, and he cannot understand them, because they are spiritually discerned. 15 The spiritual man makes judgments about all things, but he himself is not subject to

any man's judgment: 16 "For who has known the mind of the Lord that he may instruct him?" But we have the mind of Christ. NIV

The Holy Spirit of God provides guidance through discernment, understanding, discipline, revelation, and protection. God reveals Himself to us based on our level of spiritual maturity. An earthly father wouldn't expect his eight-year-old child to start managing the family business. However, once the child's level of understanding and maturity become evident, then the father would begin grooming his child accordingly.

Your Heavenly Father has a plan and a roll for you to fulfill as well:

Ephesians 2:10
For we are His workmanship, created in Christ Jesus for good works, which God prepared beforehand that we should walk in them. NKJV

Christians should also reflect the Spirit of God in our new lives by displaying the fruit of the Spirit. Here are the verses that show the differences between the spirit of the world and the Spirit of God:

Galatians 5:19-25
19 The acts of the sinful nature are obvious: sexual immorality, impurity and debauchery; 20 idolatry and witchcraft; hatred, discord, jealousy, fits of rage, selfish ambition, dissensions, factions 21 and envy; drunkenness, orgies, and the like. I warn you, as I did before, that those who live like this will not inherit the kingdom of God. 22 But the fruit of the Spirit is love, joy, peace, patience, kindness, goodness, faithfulness, 23 gentleness and self-control. Against such things there is no law.

24 Those who belong to Christ Jesus have crucified the sinful nature with its passions and desires. 25 Since we live by the Spirit, let us keep in step with the Spirit. NIV

Not only has God given us the fruit of His Spirit, He has also given each of us spiritual gifts for our unique role within the family of God. As for now, I pray that your knowledge of the Lord will cause your love for Him and people to grow stronger day by day. In order for you to grow spiritually, it is vitally important to spend time with God and to be in His Word daily. You would not be very healthy if you only ate food once or twice a week. God desires for His children to know Him intimately. For a relationship to develop and grow, you spend as much time as you possibly can with that person. It is the same with God. I recommend a morning quiet-time with prayer, Bible reading, and journaling. **MAKE TIME** for just you and the Lord to spend together. As a guideline, I like to have my quiet-time with God before the hustle and bustle of the day begins and there are no distractions. It is like putting on your armor *before* going into battle instead of when you return home from battle. An example of a morning quiet-time looks something like this:

Open in prayer: Begin by thanking God for all of your blessings. We should always have an attitude of humility and gratitude when praying to God. Pray for others in your life who are going through illnesses, relationship struggles, etc. Pray for family or friends who still need salvation. Pray that God would open a door for the gospel by preparing their hearts beforehand. Pray also for your church family and leaders, civic and national leaders, and our armed forces and their families. Pray for personal spiritual growth and understanding of God and His Word. Pray for direction, protection, and wisdom. Talk to God in a respectful, honest manner. Just repeating the "Lord's Prayer" for the sake of saying it, or repeating a "poem prayer" doesn't establish an intimate relationship that you should be seeking with your Heavenly Father.

Reading God's Word: For a new believer, I always like to start them reading the Gospel of John in the New Testament. Try to read only one or two chapters at a time because you will want to meditate on what you read throughout the day. Remember, King David hid God's Word in his heart so that he wouldn't sin against God. That should be every Christian's goal. It is also important to have **quality** Bible time. Don't just speed read so that you can check Bible time off your list for the day.

If you can do so, read your Bible, both in the morning and in the evening just before bedtime. I may read a few of the Psalms and Proverbs in the Old Testament. I like to pray and meditate on what I have read as I am drifting off to sleep. Try not to get too bogged down in Old Testament genealogies and things that are difficult to understand when first starting out. I would recommend starting with the New Testament along with Psalms and Proverbs in the O.T. Please find a good translation that you can read and understand. The King James Version is good, but many find it hard to understand the old English. For the most part, I use either the New King James Version (NKJV) or the New American Standard Version (NASV). These translations are really close word-for-word translations that I trust. I also use the New International Version on occasion.

Journaling your experience: After you spend some time in prayer and in the Word, take a moment to write down some of your thoughts. Be sure to put the date on the page. Use a journal or notebook to jot down things such as answered prayers, things that you learned about God that day, something that you learned about yourself, etc. Over a period of just a few weeks or months of consistent quiet-time and journaling, you will be amazed at your spiritual progress as you read back through your journal.

Remember, God told His people through the prophet Hosea that they are destroyed from a lack of knowledge. The knowledge that God was referring to was about Him. So why are God's people destroyed from a lack of the knowledge of God? Simple answer:

1 Peter 5:8
Be sober; be vigilant; because your adversary the devil walks about like a roaring lion, seeking whom he may devour. NKJV

Closing Thoughts:

Jesus will meet you where you are spiritually and help you along the way. In fact, Jesus summed it up for us when He was asked which of the Commandments was the greatest:

Mark 12:29-31
29 Jesus answered him, "The first of all the command-ments is: 'Hear, O Israel, the LORD our God, the LORD is one. 30 And you shall love the LORD your God with all your heart, with all your soul, with all your mind, and with all your strength.' This is the first commandment. 31 And the second, like it, is this: 'You shall love your neighbor as yourself.' There is no other commandment greater than these." NKJV

So we do not have to know everything there is to know about the Bible to love God and each other. Love for God, however, is displayed through action and obedience. Always remember what God has done for you and live your life in such a way that honors Him and brings Him glory. Many people today do not have a healthy, reverent fear and under-standing of God. Just like electricity, God has laws that, when violated, can lead to death. Electricity is impersonal and without grace. God, however, is personal, loving, and full of grace.

When I was a young boy, the words that I dreaded hearing the most coming from my mother's mouth were: "Young man, you just wait until your father gets home." If I received discipline, it was because I knew the rules, ignored the warnings, and continued down my path of rebellion. If I received grace, it was because I was truly repentant and promised to behave according to the rules that were in place for my protection. You have to **know** what God expects before you can **obey** God. However, just knowing what God expects does not substitute for obedience. Furthermore, just because God may choose to show us grace instead of discipline, that grace doesn't always excuse us from the consequences of our actions.

Things to Consider:

1. Name the six stages of a Christian's spiritual growth found at the beginning of this chapter.

2. In **2 Peter 1:2-11** what are the seven qualities that we should add to our faith in increasing measure so that we do not become ineffective and unproductive in our knowledge of Jesus Christ our Lord?

3. In **Psalm 119:11**, where did King David treasure God's Word? Why?

4. Why is knowledge of God and His Word so important?

5. Why do you think that a parent starts teaching their children things so early?

6. Will you commit to **MAKE** time at the start of your day for a quiet-time with God? When?

CHAPTER FIVE

<u>Living</u> the Word of God

John 10:10
The thief does not come except to steal, and to kill, and to destroy. I have come that they may have life, and that they may have it more abundantly. NKJV

*T*here are major differences between those who are born-again into the Kingdom of God and those who are still deceived by Satan. Besides becoming a new creature in Christ, Christians have purpose and hope as opposed to the futile life that we lived before Christ. Now we are disciples of Jesus and have begun to read His Word and be led by the Holy Spirit. In the previous chapter, we covered the importance of what it means to "know" what God says and expects of us as His children. "Living the Word" is the second part of your spiritual growth process on your KLS-WES journey. Knowing what God expects isn't enough. We must be good stewards of what we know so that we can live life abundantly and blessed. So what does the "abundant" life look like?

Before a person is saved, their definition of abundant living would probably include just about everything that you could buy with money. We do not ever have to worry about our Heavenly Father providing for us. Look at what Jesus had to say about this before we move forward:

Matthew 6:25-33

25 "Therefore I say to you, do not worry about your life, what you will eat or what you will drink; nor about your body, what you will put on. Is not life more than food and the body more than clothing? 26 Look at the birds of the air, for they neither sow nor reap nor gather into barns; yet your heavenly Father feeds them. Are you not of more value than they? 27 Which of you by worrying can add one cubit to his stature? 28 So why do you worry about clothing? Consider the lilies of the field, how they grow: they neither toil nor spin; 29 and yet I say to you that even Solomon in all his glory was not arrayed like one of these. 30 Now if God so clothes the grass of the field, which today is, and tomorrow is thrown into the oven, will He not much more clothe you, O you of little faith? 31 Therefore do not worry, saying, 'What shall we eat?' or 'What shall we drink?' or 'What shall we wear?' 32 For after all these things the Gentiles seek. For your heavenly Father knows that you need all these things. 33 But seek first the kingdom of God and His righteousness, and all these things shall be added to you." NKJV

The sad thing for many Americans is that we think that we have to live above our means. This gets us into debt and brings about all kinds of troubles that God never intended for us to have. Not having a materialistic mindset can free a person of many troubles.

There are twelve things that I believe every new Christian should understand right up front. As a new Christian begins to understand and embrace these twelve concepts, spiritual fruit will also become evident in their lives:

1) *2 Corinthians 5:7 We live by faith, not by sight.* NIV
2) Total surrender to God. Part-time Christianity does NOT work.
3) Forgive others as the Lord has forgiven you. Leave no room for bitterness.
4) God blesses obedience and disciplines His disobedient children.
5) God expects and blesses good stewardship.
6) Learn to be content. Needs and wants are different.
7) Patience and prayer pay off.
8) Our spiritual armor is for 24/7 use.
9) God loves a cheerful giver.
10) Trials and tests build character and refine our faith.
11) God has blessed us with spiritual gifts for serving others.
12) **1 Corinthians 10:31** *So whether you eat or drink or whatever you do, do it all for the glory of God.* NIV

I purposely left out most of the verses that support these twelve things because I want you to do something. Copy this list down and keep it in your Bible. As you read and study God's Word, write down all the Scripture references that you find for each number as you find them. For instance, **Hebrews 11:6** is one verse that would go with #1. **John 17:4** is a verse that could go with #12. You will soon discover that these twelve things are continually reoccurring in your Bible. This is not an exhaustive list of things that a Christian should know, but it is a great starting place.

God expects His children to conform to His Word and bond together in one Spirit.

Ephesians 4:1-6

I, therefore, the prisoner of the Lord, beseech you to walk worthy of the calling with which you were called, 2 with all lowliness and gentleness, with longsuffering, bearing with one another in love, 3 endeavoring to keep the unity of the Spirit in the bond of peace. 4 There is one body and one Spirit, just as you were called in one hope of your calling; 5 one Lord, one faith, one baptism; 6 one God and Father of all, who is above all, and through all, and in you all. NKJV

As you read through the gospels, and further into the New Testament, notice how some of the first disciples of Christ changed as they matured in their faith. Peter is an excellent example. He was just a local fisherman who loved the Lord, but would constantly say all the wrong things. However, as we follow his spiritual journey, Peter matured into an apostle who helped get the early church started and thriving. Peter's spiritual journey gives hope to someone like me who can identify with Peter's foot-in-mouth syndrome. In fact, all Christians have a purpose and destiny according to the spiritual gifts they receive.

Ephesians 2:10
For we are His workmanship, created in Christ Jesus for good works, which God prepared beforehand that we should walk in them. NKJV

So living out God's Word as we learn it prepares us for the good works that we have been set apart for in Christ Jesus.

Since we are now disciples of Jesus, it is important to understand how Jesus defines *His* disciples:

John 8:31
". . . If you abide in My word, you are My disciples indeed." NKJV

John 13:34-35

34 "A new commandment I give to you, that you love one another, even as I have loved you, that you also love one another. 35 By this all men will know that you are My disciples, if you have love for one another." NASU

John 15:8

"My Father is glorified by this, that you bear much fruit, and so prove to be My disciples." NASU

Many people may claim to be a disciple of Jesus. However, we must embrace and embody the definitions that Jesus gave us to truly be His disciples. By knowing and abiding in His Word, we will be able to love others and produce much fruit as His disciples.

1 John 2:5-6

5 But whoever keeps His word, truly the love of God is perfected in him. By this we know that we are in Him. 6 He who says he abides in Him ought himself also to walk just as He walked. NKJV

John 15:1-11

"I am the true vine, and My Father is the vinedresser. 2 Every branch in Me that does not bear fruit He takes away; and every branch that bears fruit He prunes, that it may bear more fruit. 3 You are already clean because of the word which I have spoken to you. 4 Abide in Me, and I in you. As the branch cannot bear fruit of itself, unless it abides in the vine, neither can you, unless you abide in Me.

5 I am the vine, you are the branches. He who abides in Me, and I in him, bears much fruit; for without Me you can do nothing. 6 If anyone does not abide in Me, he is cast out as a branch and is withered; and they gather them and throw them into the fire, and they are burned. 7 If you abide in Me, and My words abide in you, you will ask what you desire, and it shall be done for you. 8 By this My Father is glorified, that you bear much fruit; so you will be My disciples. 9 As the Father loved Me, I also have loved you; abide in My love. 10 If you keep My commandments, you will abide in My love, just as I have kept My Father's commandments and abide in His love. 11 These things I have spoken to you, that My joy may remain in you, and that your joy may be full." NKJV

So clearly, apart from abiding in Christ and His Word, we can do nothing for the Kingdom of God. Loving God and obeying God are one in the same:

John 14:15
"If you love Me, keep My commandments." NKJV

Luke 6:46-49
46 "Why do you call me, 'Lord, Lord,' and do not do what I say? 47 I will show you what he is like who comes to me and hears my words and puts them into practice. 48 He is like a man building a house, who dug down deep and laid the foundation on rock. When a flood came, the torrent struck that house but could not shake it, because it was well built. 49 But the one who hears my words and does not put them into practice is like a man who built a house on the ground without a foundation. The moment the torrent struck that house, it collapsed and its destruction was complete." NIV

James 1:22
22 But be doers of the word, and not hearers only, deceiving yourselves. NKJV

As the verses above point out, it's not enough to just know what God says, we actually have to practice it in our daily lives. Life and blessings come from obedience. Discipline and/or death result from continued disobedience. Remember, we do have an adversary (Satan) that seeks to kill, steal, and destroy. God's Word has been given to us because of His love for us. It is also for our protection, correction, spiritual growth, and blessings.

2 Timothy 3:16-17
16 All Scripture is given by inspiration of God, and is profitable for doctrine, for reproof, for correction, for instruction in righteousness, 17 that the man of God may be complete, thoroughly equipped for every good work. NKJV

In order to live an effective Christian life, we must always remember that we are in a continual state of spiritual warfare against Satan and the forces of darkness. As discussed in chapter three of this book, Satan's goal is to suppress the truth, and the knowledge of God, from people. You will be under daily attack by evil forces in order to render you ineffective for the Kingdom of God. So as a reminder, never take off your spiritual armor. God provided it for a reason. No soldier whom I am aware of will go into battle without all the protection and arsenal that he can carry. You have to have the mindset of a spiritual warrior every day, always on the lookout and ready for attack from the enemy. Beware; the enemy always waits until you are in vulnerable moments to attack. No, he does not fight fair.

More often than not, Christians allow themselves to become voluntarily vulnerable. This can occur when we allow any one of the following to take place in our lives:

- We become slack in wearing our spiritual armor.
- We are not reading and meditating on God's Word on a daily basis.
- We are out of fellowship with God and/or our brothers and sisters in Christ.
- We are harboring bitterness and/or unforgiveness.
- We are harboring unconfessed sin in our lives.
- We lose focus of our mission to win the lost for Christ.
- When we ignore and grieve the Holy Spirit.
- When we are not correctable or teachable because of pride and arrogance.
- When we stray from sound doctrine.
- When we do not pray as we should.

Satan will stop at nothing to make you ineffective and unproductive in your Christian walk. He will discredit your witness, if at all possible. We should always remember what Jesus did for us on the cross so that we could be free from the penalty of our sins. In doing so, we should do everything within our power not to show contempt for the grace and salvation God has given us. Always remember:

1 Corinthians 6:20
For you were bought at a price; therefore glorify God in your body and in your spirit, which are God's. NKJV

Ephesians 5:8-11
8 For you were once darkness, but now you are light in the Lord. Live as children of light 9(for the fruit of the light consists in all goodness, righteousness and truth) 10 and find out what pleases the Lord. 11 Have nothing to do with the fruitless deeds of darkness, but rather expose them. NIV

Spiritual attacks will happen just about every day for the rest of your earthly journey as a Christian. It is important for all Christians to have brothers and sisters in the faith that we are accountable to so that we can make it through the tougher battles. We are not to go this journey alone, but arm-in-arm with our brothers and sisters in the faith.

Your desire to live a holy life will also be subject to persecution. It comes standard as part of Satan's hatred of mankind and those who belong to the family of God.

2 Timothy 3:12
Yes, and all who desire to live godly in Christ Jesus will suffer persecution. NKJV

John 15:18-20
18 "If the world hates you, keep in mind that it hated me first. 19 If you belonged to the world, it would love you as its own. As it is, you do not belong to the world, but I have chosen you out of the world. That is why the world hates you. 20 Remember the words I spoke to you: 'No servant is greater than his master.' If they persecuted me, they will persecute you also. If they obeyed my teaching, they will obey yours also." NIV

The world will ridicule and despise you for who you are in Christ. It will try to pull you back into the same mess from which Jesus rescued you. In fact, there are many "professing" Christians who sit on the fence. They keep one foot in the world and one foot in Christianity. Well, the truth is, Satan owns the fence.

Luke 9:62
But Jesus said to him, "No one, after putting his hand to the plow and looking back, is fit for the kingdom of God." NASU

Even though our family, jobs, finances, health, minds, etc., may come under attack, we should never forget our identity in Christ. We do not have to live in fear and doubt any longer. The world looks at the size of the storm and is overcome with fear. Christians should understand the size and love of their God and overcome fear with faith, God's Word, praise, worship, and thanksgiving.

1 John 4:4

You are from God, little children, and have overcome them; because greater is He who is in you than he who is in the world. NASU

Isaiah 54:17

"No weapon formed against you shall prosper,
And every tongue which rises against you in judgment
You shall condemn. This is the heritage of the servants
of the LORD,
And their righteousness is from Me,"
Says the LORD. NKJV

Romans 8:31

What then shall we say to these things? If God is for us, who can be against us? NKJV

Romans 8:37

Yet in all these things we are more than conquerors through Him who loved us. NKJV

A six-year-old girl or a ninety-year-old lady can accomplish as much through prayer, fasting, and spiritual warfare as a well-equipped army of preachers. God tilts the battlefield in our favor. In spiritual warfare, one plus God equals a majority. The Word of God, prayer, fasting, AND accountability are essential to victorious Christian living.

Remember the following verses the next time you are undergoing temptation:

1 Corinthians 10:13
No temptation has overtaken you except such as is common to man; but God is faithful, who will not allow you to be tempted beyond what you are able, but with the temptation will also make the way of escape, that you may be able to bear it. NKJV

James 4:7-8
7 "Submit yourselves, then, to God. Resist the devil, and he will flee from you. 8 Come near to God and he will come near to you. . ." NIV

As part of the ongoing spiritual war between God and Satan, God's people will always endure hate and hardships in this world. Persecution will be perpetrated against all who take a stand for Christ by those who are deceived by Satan. *However, Christians need to understand that whatever our earthly circumstances may be, we have a purpose and a mission to live out.* Paul spent much time in prison. But Paul was obedient while he was there and wrote much of the New Testament by inspiration of the Holy Spirit. He also shared the gospel with his captors and led some to Christ. God is sovereign and will place His people strategically for maximum effect against the forces of darkness. That is why it is so important that Christians keep their focus on their purpose: KLS-WES. (Know it, Live it, Share it, so you can Win, Equip, and Send others to do the same.

2 Corinthians 1:3-5
3 Praise be to the God and Father of our Lord Jesus Christ, the Father of compassion and the God of all comfort, 4 who comforts us in all our troubles, so that

we can comfort those in any trouble with the comfort we ourselves have received from God. 5 For just as the sufferings of Christ flow over into our lives, so also through Christ our comfort overflows. NIV

Our total surrender to God's plan will always do the most good for the Kingdom of God. Father knows best.

If you can allow the joy that you receive to overflow to others with love, hope and compassion, you will advance the Kingdom of God by your obedient, joyful lifestyle. You will be the 'light on the hill' spoken of by Jesus in Matthew, chapter 5 that leads others to Himself. But if you let the world get you down, and you stay down, then you will become ineffective and unfruitful for the Kingdom of God. This actually helps the enemy advance his agenda.

Matthew 5:11-16

11 "Blessed are you when they revile and persecute you, and say all kinds of evil against you falsely for My sake. 12 Rejoice and be exceedingly glad, for great is your reward in heaven, for so they persecuted the prophets who were before you.

13 You are the salt of the earth; but if the salt loses its flavor, how shall it be seasoned? It is then good for nothing but to be thrown out and trampled underfoot by men. 14 You are the light of the world. A city that is set on a hill cannot be hidden. 15 Nor do they light a lamp and put it under a basket, but on a lamp stand, and it gives light to all who are in the house. 16 Let your light so shine before men, that they may see your good works and glorify your Father in heaven." NKJV

Hebrews 12:1-3
Therefore, since we are surrounded by such a great cloud of witnesses, let us throw off everything that hinders and the sin that so easily entangles, and let us run with perseverance the race marked out for us. 2 Let us fix our eyes on Jesus, the author and perfecter of our faith, who for the joy set before him endured the cross, scorning its shame, and sat down at the right hand of the throne of God. 3 Consider him who endured such opposition from sinful men, so that you will not grow weary and lose heart. NIV

All Christians should have a church where they worship and fellowship with other believers. We are ONE body with different gifts. We are also commanded not to forsake the gathering together of ourselves:

Hebrews 10:24-25
24 And let us consider how we may spur one another on toward love and good deeds. 25 Let us not give up meeting together, as some are in the habit of doing, but let us encourage one another—and all the more as you see the Day approaching. NIV

God also gives us spiritual gifts by which to minister to each other in various ways. Corporate or (collective) praise and worship are just as important as individual praise and worship. God, above all, is worthy of ALL praise and worship because of who He is, and what He has done for us. Jesus tells us what kind of worshippers He seeks:

John 4:23-24
23 But the hour is coming, and now is, when the true worshipers will worship the Father in spirit and truth; for the Father is seeking such to worship Him. 24 God is

Spirit, and those who worship Him must worship in spirit and truth." NKJV

Closing Thoughts:

God commands that His Children live holy lives because He is holy. As we commit to living the life worthy of our calling, we know that Jesus is always present with us. God will reward His children according to their obedience and their fruit. Your faithful stewardship of spiritual gifts and earthly means will help to further the Kingdom of God and rescue sinners. Live every day to glorify God and you won't be disappointed. I have never heard of someone on their death bed wishing that they had not served the Lord for so many years. On the contrary, the opposite is usually the case. They wished that they had begun serving the Lord much sooner in life.

Matthew 16:24-27
Then Jesus said to His disciples, "If anyone desires to come after Me, let him deny himself, and take up his cross, and follow Me. 25 For whoever desires to save his life will lose it, but whoever loses his life for My sake will find it. 26 For what profit is it to a man if he gains the whole world, and loses his own soul? Or what will a man give in exchange for his soul? 27 For the Son of Man will come in the glory of His Father with His angels, and then He will reward each according to his works." NKJV

1 Corinthians 10:31-33
31 So whether you eat or drink or whatever you do, do it all for the glory of God. 32 Do not cause anyone to stumble, whether Jews, Greeks or the church of God—33 even as I try to please everybody in every way. For I am

not seeking my own good but the good of many, so that they may be saved. NIV

Colossians 3:12-17

12 Therefore, as God's chosen people, holy and dearly loved, clothe yourselves with compassion, kindness, humility, gentleness and patience. 13 Bear with each other and forgive whatever grievances you may have against one another. Forgive as the Lord forgave you. 14 And over all these virtues put on love, which binds them all together in perfect unity. 15 Let the peace of Christ rule in your hearts, since as members of one body you were called to peace. And be thankful. 16 Let the word of Christ dwell in you richly as you teach and admonish one another with all wisdom, and as you sing psalms, hymns and spiritual songs with gratitude in your hearts to God. 17 And whatever you do, whether in word or deed, do it all in the name of the Lord Jesus, giving thanks to God the Father through him. NIV

Things to Consider:

- Before answering the following questions, please take the time to read **Romans chapter 12 and Ephesians chapter 4.**

1. How is the 'abundant life' that Jesus gave us different from the world's idea of abundant living?

2. What twelve things do I personally believe that ALL Christians should understand from the start?

3. Name three things that define a disciple of Jesus, according to Jesus.

4. Who are we to become more and more like as we mature in the Word of God?

5. Why are Christians under continual attack by the forces of evil?

6. What has God given us to defend and stand against Satan's attacks?

7. Why is it important to attend a Bible believing / teaching church regularly?

8. What did you study in your quiet time this morning? What did you learn?

9. List three things that you learned from Romans chapter 12.

10. List three things that you learned from Ephesians chapter 4.

CHAPTER SIX

A Lifestyle of <u>Sharing</u> the Gospel

❋

*J*esus gave instructions in the "Great Commission" to His followers (**Matthew 28: 18-20**) to "make disciples of all nations." Here is the catch; you have to be a disciple of Christ in order to reproduce, or make other disciples of Christ. One must be born again by the Spirit of God in order to effectively teach another believer how to lead someone else to Christ.

Mark 16:15-16
15 And He said to them, "Go into all the world and preach the gospel to every creature. 16 He who believes and is baptized will be saved; but he who does not believe will be condemned." NKJV

Salvation is the best thing that any person could ever experience. It is that moment when you realize that your sins have been forgiven and washed away by the blood of Jesus. It is knowing that you are no longer under the condemnation and wrath of God, but you can now call the Creator of the universe: "Abba" or Father. You now have a new life, complete with the Holy Spirit of God within you. Your eternal destination has changed from Hell to Heaven in an instant.

So, if salvation is the best thing that can ever happen to a person, why aren't more Christians actively sharing their faith? Think about that for a moment. We can't wait to share with our friends and family about a good movie that we have seen. In most cases, we share all the good things that we experience on earth *except* for our faith. So why do we not share the most important thing in our life? Are we ashamed of our God or the salvation that we have? Notice what Jesus had to say in regard to being ashamed of Him:

Luke 9:26
For whoever is ashamed of Me and My words, of him the Son of Man will be ashamed when He comes in His own glory, and in His Father's, and of the holy angels. NKJV

On the other hand, maybe we don't share our faith because we are overtaken by fear. Fear of rejection, persecution, offending someone, or just being afraid because we don't know what to say. These are feelings that most Christians deal with on a regular basis. Did you know that even the apostle Paul asked for prayer so that he would be bold in presenting the gospel?

Ephesians 6:19-20
19 Pray also for me, that whenever I open my mouth, words may be given me so that I will fearlessly make known the mystery of the gospel, 20 for which I am an ambassador in chains. Pray that I may declare it fearlessly, as I should. NIV

The early Christians were really no different in that they needed God's help to deal with fear and other obstacles. God answered their prayers and a few dedicated, Spirit-filled Christians turned the world upside down for Christ. As you proceed through this chapter, may God open your heart for the lost like never before. Sharing the gospel of Jesus Christ should be something that every Christian looks forward to doing at every opportunity. In fact, we have many opportunities to share our faith all the time. We just need to open our eyes and our hearts.

How we live our lives and treat those who are not born-again makes all the difference in the world. Do you, as a Christian, live differently than those who are lost? If you were arrested for being a Christian, would there be enough evidence to convict you? Many people who profess to be Christians live their lives with little or no difference than the world. It is hard to convince someone that they need a Savior when *your* life is no different than those you are trying to reach. People need to see the light and hope in you before they want what you have in their own life.

1 Peter 3:15-17

15 But sanctify the Lord God in your hearts, and always be ready to give a defense to everyone who asks you a reason for the hope that is in you, with meekness and fear; 16 having a good conscience, that when they defame you as evildoers, those who revile your good conduct in Christ may be ashamed. 17 For it is better, if it is the will of God, to suffer for doing good than for doing evil. NKJV

Colossians 4:5-6

5 Walk in wisdom toward those who are outside, redeeming the time. 6 Let your speech always be with grace, seasoned with salt, that you may know how you ought to answer each one. NKJV

All of God's children should be living their lives in such a way that glorifies Him. Remember, we are salt and light. So many Christians never understand that they are a light for deceived captives in a lost, dark world. We shine brightly in church and then cover our light when we go out into the darkness (our mission field). Even though we are salt and light, don't expect those trapped in the darkness of sin to flock toward you. Light exposes things that darkness hides. Some will run from the light because of their shame and rebellion. Some, however, will come into the light because it gives them hope from their depraved state of existence.

Most people are naturally drawn to those who are joyful and full of light and life. Many people are turned off by negative grumblers who are full of darkness and doom. If you are going to be an effective witness for the gospel, you are going to have to uncover your light and let it shine outside the church walls. Some will not like it. However, let us not forget who we are and that our mission is to rescue the lost from the grip of Satan.

Acts 26:18
18 to open their eyes, in order to turn them from darkness to light, and from the power of Satan to God, that they may receive forgiveness of sins and an inheritance among those who are sanctified by faith in Me. NKJV

Here are a few things to consider in regard to sharing your faith with the lost:

1) Remember that it was by the love, power, and grace of God that you were saved. Your spiritual eyes were opened when the Truth (Jesus) set you free. The lost remain deceived by Satan, and the message of the cross is foolishness to them.

1 Corinthians 1:18

For the message of the cross is foolishness to those who are perishing, but to us who are being saved it is the power of God. NIV

2) Intercessory prayer and fasting are key to breaking strongholds that keep captives from the knowledge of God. Whether you are praying for one person or a country, you should always pray that God would go before you and soften hearts and minds to receive the gospel message. It is like a farmer who prepares his field before planting the seeds. The better prepared the field, the better chance the seeds have to take root. Prayer, fasting, and the FULL armor of God are mandatory equipment when sharing your faith. Satan does not let his captives go willingly. **Soul winning IS spiritual warfare.**

3) Be yourself and share your testimony of how you got saved. You should always be prepared to do this since you never forget how and when you were saved. It is important to remember that your story matters, no matter how insignificant you think it is to others. Try to keep your testimony as short as possible. There are many distractions, such as cell phones, that can interrupt your message. God will strategically position His people where He needs them to accomplish His Will at any given time. **Only won souls win souls.**

4) We actually have to proclaim the gospel to the lost. While living a holy life is important, actually sharing the gospel is a must. People need to hear both the good news and the bad news. The bad news, of course, is spending eternity in Hell without salva-

tion. This serves as a warning and makes the good news better news.

2 Timothy 4:2
Preach the Word; be prepared in season and out of season; correct, rebuke and encourage—with great patience and careful instruction. NIV

Romans 10:17
So then faith comes by hearing, and hearing by the word of God. NKJV

You are only responsible for sharing your faith and the gospel. You are not responsible for people's reaction to your message. Remember that Jesus said:

Matthew 7:13-14
13 "Enter through the narrow gate. For wide is the gate and broad is the road that leads to destruction, and many enter through it. 14 But small is the gate and narrow the road that leads to life, and only a few find it." NIV

Sadly, according to the verses above, there will be many more who reject your message than will accept the good news of the gospel. Just like a smoke alarm on the wall, after it has sounded the alarm, it has done its job. It is not responsible for people's reaction to its warning. At this time, please read **Ezekiel 33:1-9** in your Bible. There will be questions over these verses at the end of this chapter.

5) There is no substitute for being prepared. Make it a point to learn something new from the Word of God every day. A soldier trains hard every day to be prepared for whatever the enemy might try. Christians should be no different. We should be prepared for

action in living out our faith and serving others. We should be prepared when it is convenient and when it is not. **We should be prepared to witness to others by words and good deeds.**

1 Peter 1:13
Therefore, prepare your minds for action; be self-controlled; set your hope fully on the grace to be given you when Jesus Christ is revealed. NIV

Titus 3:14
And let our people also learn to maintain good works, to meet urgent needs, that they may not be unfruitful. NKJV

James 2:26
For as the body without the spirit is dead, so faith without works is dead also. NKJV

6) The gospel has certain components that make it the gospel. These doctrinal truths should be included and not omitted when presenting the gospel message. These things include Heaven, Hell, repentance, the cross, the atoning shed blood of Jesus for sins, the love of God, forgiveness, etc. It is easy to cut corners, but unless the lost person has the whole story, they are not making a decision for Heaven or Hell based on all the facts. Sound doctrine is essential when sharing our faith, living our faith, and discipling others in the faith. The closer we get to the end times, the harder it will be to win souls. "Religion" may have left a sour taste in the mouth of many people. They may have never heard of the good news of the gospel that offers true salvation.

1 Timothy 4:15-16

15 Be diligent in these matters; give yourself wholly to them, so that everyone may see your progress. 16 Watch your life and doctrine closely. Persevere in them, because if you do, you will save both yourself and your hearers. NIV

2 Timothy 4:3-5

3 For the time will come when men will not put up with sound doctrine. Instead, to suit their own desires, they will gather around them a great number of teachers to say what their itching ears want to hear. 4 They will turn their ears away from the truth and turn aside to myths. 5 But you, keep your head in all situations, endure hardship, do the work of an evangelist, discharge all the duties of your ministry. NIV

Titus 2:1

You must teach what is in accord with sound doctrine. NIV

So as you can see, sound doctrine is important, not only for sharing your faith, but for living and discipleship as well. Satan began twisting the Word of God in the Garden of Eden, and he hasn't stopped since.

We should have the same love and concern for the lost that God has for them. The things that break God's heart should break ours as well. The world needs to know that we genuinely care for their spiritual and physical well-being. It is important to understand that deceived people don't know they are deceived any more than sleeping people know that they are asleep. They only realize both when their eyes have been opened.

In many of my past witnessing experiences, I would ask the person that I was sharing with about their spiritual background. Then, I would ask them to define a Christian.

The answer given here removes all doubt as to whether they are saved or lost. Don't be satisfied with someone just saying that they are a Christian. A true Christian will have a testimony describing how they came to know the Lord and became born again. Jesus defines a Christian this way:

John 3:3-8
3 In reply Jesus declared, "I tell you the truth, no one can see the kingdom of God unless he is born again."

4 "How can a man be born when he is old?" Nicodemus asked. "Surely he cannot enter a second time into his mother's womb to be born!"

5 Jesus answered, "I tell you the truth, no one can enter the kingdom of God unless he is born of water and the Spirit. 6 Flesh gives birth to flesh, but the Spirit gives birth to spirit. 7 You should not be surprised at my saying, 'You must be born again.' 8 The wind blows wherever it pleases. You hear its sound, but you cannot tell where it comes from or where it is going. So it is with everyone born of the Spirit." NIV

So it is okay to dig deeper to understand what the person that you are sharing with understands about being a Christian. Their eternity may depend on you sharing the truth. When I would show the person these verses and ask them when they were born again, they usually couldn't tell me. Or, they would proudly explain how they grew up in church. So I would share the good news of the gospel with them. Some would believe, and some were content believing their version of Christianity instead of God's version. That is a sad reality that we must endure as we proclaim the truth. Nevertheless, for those who believe and receive salvation, it means eternity with the Lord.

Closing Thoughts:

Often, Christians forget that we are being closely watched by those we are trying to reach for the gospel. Our walk and our talk should match; and both should line up with our Christian faith. I pinched my finger while working on a machine once and said something that I should not have said. One person came over to me and stated that he thought that I was a Christian. That one incident really alerted me to the great cloud of witnesses that surround us at any given time. I have learned that it is just as easy to proclaim: "Jesus saves sinners" when I hurt myself rather than cursing and swearing. Living our life in such a way that the lost want what we have is the goal. Make sure that you are a light in the darkness for others to find Christ. Running with the wrong crowd will not help your witness.

1 Corinthians 15:33-34
33 Do not be misled: "Bad company corrupts good character." 34 Come back to your senses as you ought, and stop sinning; for there are some who are ignorant of God—I say this to your shame. NIV

Things to Consider:

1. What are some possible reasons why some Christians don't share their faith?

2. Why does it matter that Christians live differently than those they are trying to reach with the gospel?

3. What did you learn from **Ezekiel 33:1-9**?

4. What definition of a Christian did Jesus give in **John 3:3-8**?

Components of the Great Commission

Matthew 28:18-20

18 And Jesus came and spoke to them, saying, "All authority has been given to Me in heaven and on earth. 19 Go therefore and make disciples of all the nations, baptizing them in the name of the Father and of the Son and of the Holy Spirit, 20 teaching them to observe all things that I have commanded you; and lo, I am with you always, even to the end of the age." Amen. NKJV

We clearly see that we have been commissioned to: *Go to all nations and make disciples; baptize them in the name of the Father, Son and Holy Spirit; and to teach them to obey all that Jesus has taught us to obey.* So how much of the "Great Commission" did you fulfill today? How about yesterday? Usually, this is where all the excuses will begin to flow. Many excuses stem from being too busy. Others are distracted by the cares and troubles of the world. However, there are some excuses that place the blame squarely on the back of the modern church.

Many churches are good about getting "members" whether they are born again or not. They are interested in numbers and pew warmers. Some "churches" have become no more than Sunday morning social clubs. They are great at fund-raising and building projects. They are also experts at initiating programs and forming committees. In fact, many churches don't even have pastors that are born again. I grew up in a church like this. Bible stories are good to know; however, I never heard the gospel presentation once during my twenty-two years of going to that church. Then, a complete stranger shared the good news with me in a diner. I changed churches and got baptized. They had a discipleship program where I began to learn about God and what He expects from His children. I soon begin to understand that there are many churches that do not live out the Great Commission as their main goal of furthering the Kingdom of Christ. Don't assume anything when sharing the gospel with someone. They may know all the right terminology, but not the Savior.

The Great Commission not only includes making disciples, but also baptizing and teaching them all that we have been taught. Subsequently, they are prepared and equipped to go do the same. That is KLS-WES at its core. **So the Great Commission is not just about winning converts; it is also about baptizing, and discipleship training.** It is sad that many churches only focus on making converts and not disciples. This results in spiritual babes in Christ having to raise themselves the best that they can. Usually, this results in weak doctrinal health, spiritually speaking. And, in light of the Parable of the Seeds found in **Matthew 13:3-9**, many of these converts will simply wither and fall away at the slightest hardship or inconvenience. Discipleship is just as important as making disciples. Training new disciples of Christ is like raising newborns; you don't just let newborn babies fend for themselves. All babies need to be fed until they learn how to feed themselves. All babies need milk until they are ready for solid food. The patience that God has demonstrated with you is the same patience that we should show others during this process.

So Christians are fulfilling the Great Commission, whether they are sharing the gospel, or baptizing and/or discipling other Christians. This is a life-long process for all Christians. The Apostle Paul not only established churches on his missionary journeys, but he wrote letters meant to disciple those in the churches that he established. Many of those letters are included in the New Testament of our Bible. Not only did Paul share his faith; he personally discipled many of those who received the gospel.

Christians must always use the Word of God when witnessing or discipling. The Word of God accomplishes much more than our words. Consider these familiar verses about God's Word:

Hebrews 4:12
For the word of God is living and powerful, and sharper than any two-edged sword, piercing even to the division of soul and spirit, and of joints and marrow, and is a discerner of the thoughts and intents of the heart. NKJV

Isaiah 55:11
So shall My word be that goes forth from My mouth;
It shall not return to Me void,
But it shall accomplish what I please,
And it shall prosper in the thing for which I sent it. NKJV

The Word of God encompasses everything that the Father, Son, and Holy Spirit said in either the Old or New Testament. Therefore, the Holy Bible IS the Word of God. Our words simply do not have the power to accomplish what God's Word can accomplish.

That is why it is vitally important when sharing the gospel to use Scripture as much as possible. God's Word convicts and goes deeper than our words ever could.

- I have included in the back of this book, "Appendix A" and "Appendix B." "Appendix A" can be used as a gospel tract, or a witness training tool. "Appendix B" includes references to other resources which contain effective presentation styles that I feel cover all the basis of gospel presentation. Feel free to use these resources as needed.

Closing Thoughts:

In today's culture, the Great Commission has become more about winning converts and filling church pews than making disciples of Christ. Many churches forget the part about *teaching them to obey all that He [Jesus] has taught us*. Many new babes in Christ are simply not discipled after they become Christians and join the church. Basically, they are given a stack of bulletins to hand out on Sunday mornings and a pat on the back. It is past time for churches to re-examine the Great Commission, and their obligation to fulfill this precious task. Then church members will become thoroughly equipped for every good work. Each member should feel prepared to share the gospel, water a planted seed, lead someone to Christ, or disciple a new convert. If this isn't going on in your church, you might be attending a social club.

Things to Consider:

1. What are the "action words" or (verbs) in the Great Commission?

2. What is a common misunderstanding in regard to the Great Commission?

3. Is discipling a new Christian fulfilling the Great Commission?

4. Why is it important to use the Word of God when witnessing or discipling?

5. What part of the Great Commission have you fulfilled lately? Explain:

6. How did this chapter help you better understand sharing your faith and the Great Commission?

CHAPTER SEVEN

Winning, Equipping, and Sending

Proverbs 11:30
The fruit of the righteous is a tree of life,
And he who wins souls is wise. NKJV

2 Timothy 2:15
Be diligent to present yourself approved to God, a worker
who does not need to be ashamed, rightly dividing the
word of truth. NKJV

So far, we have looked at the first part of KLS-WES. In regard to the Word of God, we have to: "Know" it so that we can "Live" it. We have to "Live" it to be obedient and "Share" it; then we can "Win," "Equip," and "Send" others to do the same.

Jesus Christ gave the Apostle Paul his mission to win people for the Kingdom of God. In fact, Paul became passionate about it. Look at what lengths he would go to for the lost:

1 Corinthians 9:19-23

19 Though I am free and belong to no man, I make myself a slave to everyone, to win as many as possible. 20 To the Jews I became like a Jew, to win the Jews. To those under the law I became like one under the law (though I myself am not under the law), so as to win those under the law. 21 To those not having the law I became like one not having the law (though I am not free from God's law but am under Christ's law), so as to win those not having the law. 22 To the weak I became weak, to win the weak. I have become all things to all men so that by all possible means I might save some. 23 I do all this for the sake of the gospel, that I may share in its blessings. NIV

2 Corinthians 6:3-4

3 We put no stumbling block in anyone's path, so that our ministry will not be discredited. 4 Rather, as servants of God we commend ourselves in every way: in great endurance; in troubles, hardships and distresses; NIV

As you can see, Paul cared greatly about winning souls for the Kingdom of God. Paul was equally as passionate about discipleship or "equipping." As previously mentioned, many of Paul's letters to churches that he established were written by inspiration of the Holy Spirit to disciple and guide them. Many of those letters are now included in the New Testament for our benefit as well. God's Word is living and does not expire.

Sound doctrine was also extremely important to Paul. The Holy Spirit made sure that a strong foundation was laid upon which the churches could build in the coming generations. At this time, it is imperative that you read **1 Corinthians 2**. This sixteen verse chapter demonstrates how God works through His Word, His people, and His Holy Spirit to accomplish His Will.

As a Christian who disciples others, be sure that you are teaching sound doctrine according to the Word of God. As a result of not being discipled properly, there are many professing Christians today who believe unbiblical doctrines. Some of these beliefs include: Belief in evolution; some are pro-abortion; some don't believe in a literal Satan or Hell; many believe that they don't have to participate in corporate worship as part of the church; some don't believe that the Bible IS the Word of God; some claimed that they can be saved while living in a lifestyle totally contrary to the Word of God; many think that Jesus was just a good, moral person and not who He claimed to be in **John 8:58);** and many believe that all humans are God's children whether they are born again or not.

These worldly beliefs stem from two primary things: 1) The church not doing its job; and 2) The fact that we are in the times when the Scriptures say:

2 Timothy 4:3-4
3 For the time will come when they will not endure sound doctrine, but according to their own desires, because they have itching ears, they will heap up for themselves teachers; 4 and they will turn their ears away from the truth, and be turned aside to fables. NKJV

There is no shortage of ear-tickling preaching in the world today. Sin is watered down while egos are built up. Obedience and holiness fall by the wayside while health and wealth seem to be the only goals of the faith. Jesus is our example. Let's get back to following Him and His Word.

There will be many things that you run across in the Scriptures that you may not understand. It is okay to not know all the answers. There are, however, certain doctrinal truths that define Christianity that you should know. Among these are: The virgin birth of Christ; the deity of Christ; the

sinless life of Jesus; the miracles of Christ; the atoning sacrifice for our sins on the cross by His shed blood; the resurrection of Jesus on the third day; His ascension into Heaven;
the holy Trinity consisting of one God in three Persons as
the Father, Son, and Holy Spirit; a literal Heaven and Hell;
a literal Satan; The return of Christ for His church; and the
final Judgment Day.

These are eternal truths that time will not change in
regard to Christ. There is only one name by which men must
be saved and no other; the name of Jesus. If there were many
paths that lead to God, Jesus didn't have to die on the cross
for our sins. Read **Acts 4.**

Aside from those things that define Christian doctrine,
we have what I like to refer to as "in house" disagreements.
These are things that can be discussed at length with no
obvious, clear-cut answer in sight. These topics are not gen-
erally considered to be basic tenants of the faith. Rather, they
are points of interpretation that have no effect on a person's
salvation, whether they believe one way or the other. Such
things may include: Predestination vs. Freewill; Pre, Mid,
or Post Tribulation rapture of the Church; Covenant vs.
Dispensational Theology; etc. These are all considered "in
house" discussions that will not be tackled or solved within
the pages of this book. Early church father, Augustine said it
best: "In essentials – unity, in nonessentials – liberty, but in
all things – charity." This is how you should tackle all of the
arguments listed above. Remember, God is sovereign! God
does not fit into my box or your box. We just need to make
sure that we are in His box (salvation).

There are several denominations within Christianity that
adhere to one doctrine over another, but to be a "Christian"
denomination, you have to believe the essential doctrinal
truths about Christ and His Word. The mission of the church
should be to fulfill the Great Commission with love, compassion, and passion. That would include equipping the saved

and sending them out to win and equip others. It *does* matter what we teach. We will be held accountable for what we teach. Consider these words from the Scriptures:

1 Corinthians 3:1-17

3:1 Brothers, I could not address you as spiritual but as worldly—mere infants in Christ. 2 I gave you milk, not solid food, for you were not yet ready for it. Indeed, you are still not ready. 3 You are still worldly. For since there is jealousy and quarreling among you, are you not worldly? Are you not acting like mere men? 4 For when one says, "I follow Paul," and another, "I follow Apollos," are you not mere men? 5 What, after all, is Apollos? And what is Paul? Only servants, through whom you came to believe—as the Lord has assigned to each his task. 6 I planted the seed, Apollos watered it, but God made it grow. 7 So neither he who plants nor he who waters is anything, but only God, who makes things grow. 8 The man who plants and the man who waters have one purpose, and each will be rewarded according to his own labor. 9 For we are God's fellow workers; you are God's field, God's building. 10 By the grace God has given me, I laid a foundation as an expert builder, and someone else is building on it. But each one should be careful how he builds. 11 For no one can lay any foundation other than the one already laid, which is Jesus Christ. 12 If any man builds on this foundation using gold, silver, costly stones, wood, hay or straw, 13 his work will be shown for what it is, because the Day will bring it to light. It will be revealed with fire, and the fire will test the quality of each man's work. 14 If what he has built survives, he will receive his reward. 15 If it is burned up, he will suffer loss; he himself will be saved, but only as one escaping through the flames. 16 Don't you know that you yourselves are God's temple and that

God's Spirit lives in you? 17 If anyone destroys God's temple, God will destroy him; for God's temple is sacred, and you are that temple. NIV

Closing Thoughts:

Each one of us is uniquely equipped and gifted for service within the body of Christ.

Ephesians 4:11-13

11 It was he who gave some to be apostles, some to be prophets, some to be evangelists, and some to be pastors and teachers, 12 to prepare God's people for works of service, so that the body of Christ may be built up 13 until we all reach unity in the faith and in the knowledge of the Son of God and become mature, attaining to the whole measure of the fullness of Christ. NIV

Just like a well-trained army; some are skilled in combat, some in communications, some in supply and logistics, some in medical services, etc., but all are trained to work as one unit to achieve a common goal. Training should be a daily activity.

2 Timothy 2:2

And the things that you have heard from me among many witnesses, commit these to faithful men who will be able to teach others also. NKJV

The goal of discipling others is to equip them to go out and make other disciples of Christ, who will go out and do the same. This IS the mission of the church. We need to stop everything that is distracting us from that mission. We like to be spoon-fed spiritual food instead of reading and checking the Word for ourselves. How can we teach others to hear the soft, gentle voice of God if we don't take time to hear it for ourselves? Jesus promised to be with us always. We have no excuse for laziness. Souls are depending on our obedience. We need to get back into the Word of God and turn off the distractions that steal our time from God and His Word.

John 10:27
My sheep hear My voice, and I know them, and they follow Me. NKJV

Matthew 10:16
"Behold, I send you out as sheep in the midst of wolves. Therefore be wise as serpents and harmless as doves." NKJV

Romans 10:14-15
14 How, then, can they call on the one they have not believed in? And how can they believe in the one of whom they have not heard? And how can they hear without someone preaching to them? 15 And how can they preach unless they are sent? As it is written, "How beautiful are the feet of those who bring good news!" NIV

Things to Consider:

1. In 1 Corinthians 9, what did the Apostle Paul do so that he might win souls for Christ?

2. List the "essentials" of the Christian faith.

3. What did Augustine say about differences?

4. How important is sound doctrine in the Christian faith? Why?

5. What part of "KLS-WES" are you living and how will that help you fulfill the Great Commission today?

CHAPTER EIGHT

Are All Religions the Same?

*I*t seems easy enough to place all belief systems on equal ground. After all, many religions have been around almost as long as man has been on the earth. It is especially easy for people who do not practice any faith to lump all religions into one big pile of nonsense. Most religions have a code of ethics or rules which govern how their followers should live. However, in most all religions, there is usually an object (or objects) of worship. Whether the object is physical or spiritual in nature, it is a "perceived" reality to those who worship the entity. People will worship, sacrifice, and pray to their object of worship in order to earn blessings and good fortune. Fear of condemnation and punishment is also a concern if the entity in question is not appeased by the worshippers. Christians, however, believe in one God and Creator of all things. So why are there so many confusing religions?

In chapter three of this book, we took a close look at spiritual warfare and the reason that it is a reality. All through the Old Testament, there were many spiritual attacks that took place against Israel, the Chosen People of God. Satan tried several times to get God's people to pull away from God and worship someone or something else like the surrounding nations were doing. Some of the best head-to-head battles were in the Book of Exodus. One account was when God was working through Moses against the Pharaoh of Egypt to free the Israelite slaves. Read the following verses:

Exodus 7:8-13
8 Then the LORD spoke to Moses and Aaron, saying, 9 "When Pharaoh speaks to you, saying, 'Show a miracle for yourselves,' then you shall say to Aaron, 'Take your rod and cast it before Pharaoh, and let it become a serpent.'" 10 So Moses and Aaron went in to Pharaoh, and they did so, just as the LORD commanded. And Aaron cast down his rod before Pharaoh and before his servants, and it became a serpent. 11 But Pharaoh also called the wise men and the sorcerers; so the magicians of Egypt, they also did in like manner with their enchantments. 12 For every man threw down his rod, and they became serpents. But Aaron's rod swallowed up their rods. 13 And Pharaoh's heart grew hard, and he did not heed them, as the LORD had said. NKJV

God demonstrated His authority over the sorcerers and magicians who were doing their work under the power of Satan. Of course, those under Satan's power are deceived into thinking that they are doing these things by their own power, or by the power of their (gods). Either way, God is sovereign over ALL authority, earthly or otherwise. God makes it clear that He does not share His glory with any other:

Isaiah 42:8
I am the LORD, that is My name;
And My glory I will not give to another,
Nor My praise to carved images. NKJV

Now take a moment and read the twenty-five verses of: **Isaiah 45**

So far, we have seen that God does not share His glory with any part of His creation. He is sovereign over all creation. His throne is high above all other thrones or powers. There will be NO excuse for mankind if they choose to deny their Creator. Satan, since the beginning, has tried to turn human hearts away from God. Since the Devil could not stop Christ from going to the cross on our behalf, he put up many obstacles and road blocks. These were designed to confuse, deceive and control people. Unfortunately, many of the more common obstacles are false religions. These deceive people into believing anything except the biblical Jesus and His death, burial, and resurrection. Many of these are works-based religions, which mean that people have to try to earn their "salvation." Other religions include idol or earth worship. Earth and idol worship occurs when people choose to worship the created rather than the true Creator.

Romans 1:18-25

18 For the wrath of God is revealed from heaven against all ungodliness and unrighteousness of men, who suppress the truth in unrighteousness, 19 because what may be known of God is manifest in them, for God has shown it to them. 20 For since the creation of the world His invisible attributes are clearly seen, being understood by the things that are made, even His eternal power and Godhead, so that they are without excuse, 21 because, although they knew God, they did not glorify Him as God, nor were thankful, but became futile in their thoughts, and their foolish hearts were darkened. 22 Professing to be wise, they became fools, 23 and changed the glory of the incorruptible God into an image made like corruptible man—and birds and four-footed animals and creeping things. 24 Therefore God also gave them up to uncleanness, in the lusts of their hearts, to dishonor their bodies among themselves, 25 who exchanged the truth of God for the lie, and worshiped and served the creature rather than the Creator, who is blessed forever. Amen. NKJV

Satan is also called the "god" of this world, spelled with a little "g" of course. We are reminded of what the little "g" god has done to the unsaved in these verses:

2 Corinthians 4:3-4
3 But even if our gospel is veiled, it is veiled to those who are perishing, 4 whose minds the god of this age has blinded, who do not believe, lest the light of the gospel of the glory of Christ, who is the image of God, should shine on them. NKJV

Doctrines of demons, which include false christs and false prophets, are all signs of the end times spoken of by Jesus Himself. The apostle Paul even warned us that Satan can transform himself into an angel of light in order to deceive people:

2 Corinthians 11:12-15
12 But what I do, I will also continue to do, that I may cut off the opportunity from those who desire an opportunity to be regarded just as we are in the things of which they boast. 13 For such are false apostles, deceitful workers, transforming themselves into apostles of Christ. 14 And no wonder! For Satan himself transforms himself into an angel of light. 15 Therefore it is no great thing if his ministers also transform themselves into ministers of righteousness, whose end will be according to their works. NKJV

We see this occurring in many of the modern-day religions. Instead of being easily seen as a cult or false religion, some of these religions slip in under the radar by using many of the same terms as biblical Christianity. For example, Mormons, Jehovah's Witnesses, Christian Science, etc., all use many of the same terms as Christians use. So what are the two main things which separate biblical Christianity from these religions? **They are the deity of Jesus Christ, and the indwelling Holy Spirit in the born again believer.**

Romans 8:16
The Spirit himself testifies with our spirit that we are God's children. NIV

The Jesus that biblical Christians worship is NOT the brother of Lucifer as some claim. He is NOT Michael the Archangel as others suggest. Lucifer and all of the angels are created beings. **Colossians 1:15-20** makes it clear that Christ, as part of the triune Godhead, created ALL things. He is **NOT** some New Age cosmic force or impersonal being as some believe. He **IS** the only-begotten Son of the living God and second Person of the Holy Trinity of the Godhead.

1 Corinthians 8:4-6
4 Therefore concerning the eating of things offered to idols, we know that an idol is nothing in the world, and that there is no other God but one. 5 For even if there are so-called gods, whether in heaven or on earth (as there are many gods and many lords), 6 yet for us there is one God, the Father, of whom are all things, and we for Him; and one Lord Jesus Christ, through whom are all things, and through whom we live. NKJV

Jesus also made this statement during His earthly ministry:

John 14:6-7
6 Jesus said to him, "I am the way, the truth, and the life. No one comes to the Father except through Me. 7 If you had known Me, you would have known My Father also; and from now on you know Him and have seen Him." NKJV

Again, according to the Word of God, there is no other name given among men by which a person can be saved than that of Jesus (**ACTS 4:8-12**).

Paul also gives a stern warning for anyone who introduces another gospel or way of salvation except through Jesus Christ:

Galatians 1:6-9
6 I marvel that you are turning away so soon from Him who called you in the grace of Christ, to a different gospel, 7 which is not another; but there are some who trouble you and want to pervert the gospel of Christ. 8 But even if we, or an angel from heaven, preach any other gospel to you than what we have preached to you, let him be accursed. 9 As we have said before, so now I say again, if anyone preaches any other gospel to you than what you have received, let him be accursed. NKJV

Closing Thoughts:

Tolerance, diversity, and political correctness have eroded our spiritual guards in recent years to the point of accepting everything so as not to offend anyone. If nothing is sin, then we don't need a Savior. Remember, if all roads lead to the same God, then Jesus didn't have to suffer a horrible, sacrificial death on a cross for our sins. False religions are a continuation of spiritual warfare. If false religions are true, why do those who come out of that deception and become Christians agree that Christianity is the only way? Because they have encountered the indwelling Holy Spirit and the changed life that is produced as evidence. Once the truth has set a person free and opened their spiritual eyes, it is easy to see the bondage that once oppressed them.

Things to Consider:

1. Do you remember why we are commissioned to spread the good news of the gospel? (See Acts 26:18)

2. List at least 3 things that you learned about God from Isaiah 45

3. What has the "god" of this age done to those who do not believe in the gospel of Jesus Christ? (See 2 Corinthians 4:3-4)

4. What is the ONLY name given among men by which we can be saved?
(ACTS 4:8-12)

APPENDIX A

THE BIBLE

*T*he Bible is a supernatural work. It consists of sixty-six books that were written by forty, Holy Spirit inspired writers over a 1600 year period. All the books are consistent in their portrayal of God and His plan of salvation. Throughout all history, there has never been another book like it in the world. Its pages contain God's personal revelation of Himself to man via His Holy Spirit. The Bible also reveals man's depraved sin nature before a holy God; the choosing of Israel through whom the Messiah would come; God's plan to reconcile man unto Himself through His only-begotten Son, Jesus Christ; and a warning to all who choose to remain in their sins instead of being reconciled to God through the cross of Christ. The eternal rewards to be given to those who choose reconciliation and eternal life in Christ are without comparison. However, those choosing not to be reconciled to God through Jesus Christ will experience justice in the form of eternal wrath that also has no comparison. Forgiveness and salvation are free for the asking. Please choose wisely where you will spend eternity. Below are a few questions for you to consider:

Is death the end?

If not, where will I spend eternity?

How "good" do I have to be to make it to Heaven?
How do I know that God loves me?
What is salvation and why do I need it?

1. DEATH IS ONLY THE BEGINNING OF THE REST OF YOUR ETERNITY

Hebrews 9:27
And as it is appointed for men to die once, but after this the judgment, NKJV

Since God created the universe and everything in it, He also made the rules.

2. GOD ONLY PROVIDED TWO OPTIONS FOR WHERE WE WILL SPEND ETERNITY AFTER DEATH.

Matthew 25:46
And these will go away into everlasting punishment, but the righteous into eternal life. NKJV

The choices are Heaven (Eternal Life) and Hell (Eternal Punishment). Some people think that they are exempt because they do not believe in either one.

CAUTION: You do not have to believe anything to spend eternity in Hell.

3. SO HOW GOOD IS GOOD ENOUGH TO MAKE IT INTO HEAVEN?

Isaiah 64:6
All of us have become like one who is unclean, and all our righteous acts are like filthy rags; NIV

Romans 3:23
. . . for all have sinned and fall short of the glory of God, NKJV

James 2:10
For whoever keeps the whole law and yet stumbles at just one point is guilty of breaking all of it. NIV

According to the Scriptures, nobody is "good" enough by God's standards (the Ten Commandments) to earn eternal life by their own merit. Although breaking God's commandments is sin, we do not become sinners by breaking the Law, we break God's law because we are born sinners. We are born into sin because of our depraved nature. This sin-nature was what the human race inherited as the result of the fall of Adam and Eve in the Garden of Eden. In short, that means that we are all guilty of sin and sin separates us from a holy God.

4. **GOD LOVED US ENOUGH TO PAY OUR SIN PENALTY FOR US BEFORE WE EVER KNEW ANYTHING ABOUT HIM.**

John 3:16-17
For God so loved the world that He gave His only begotten Son, that whoever believes in Him should not perish but have everlasting life. 17 For God did not send His Son into the world to condemn the world, but that the world through Him might be saved. NKJV

Romans 5:8
8 But God demonstrates His own love toward us, in that while we were still sinners, Christ died for us. NKJV

So you see, God isn't trying to make people "religious." God demonstrated His love for us by sacrificing His only-begotten Son on a cross to pay for our sins. God's justice requires Him to punish sinners. Sin cannot be in His presence. Therefore, God provided a way so that we who are sinners could be forgiven and reconciled to Him.

5. SO WHAT IS SALVATION AND HOW CAN I GET IT?

Salvation is God's gift of grace, forgiveness, and eternal life to undeserving man. It is only offered through Jesus Christ. We deserve judgment and wrath, but God wants to show us mercy through forgiveness and eternal life.

Repenting (turning away) from sin is our part. This is similar to a child going to his or her parents and truly saying that they are sorry for their behavior and actions.

Acts 3:19
Repent, then, and turn to God, so that your sins may be wiped out, that times of refreshing may come from the Lord, NIV

2 Corinthians 7:10
For godly sorrow produces repentance leading to salvation, not to be regretted; but the sorrow of the world produces death. NKJV

Romans 10:9-13
9 That if you confess with your mouth, "Jesus is Lord," and believe in your heart that God raised him from the dead, you will be saved. 10 For it is with your heart that you believe and are justified, and it is with your mouth that you confess and are saved. 11 As the Scripture says, "Anyone who trusts in him will never be put to shame."

12 For there is no difference between Jew and Gentile — the same Lord is Lord of all and richly blesses all who call on him, 13 for, "Everyone who calls on the name of the Lord will be saved." NIV

Now would be a great time to repent of your sins and ask God for forgiveness and salvation. **Please don't put something that important off another minute.** Receive God's free gift of eternal live and receive His Holy Spirit just by asking Him through prayer. God wants you to belong to Him, not His enemy. Yes, He loves you that much!

John 1:12-13
12 But as many as received Him, to them He gave the right to become children of God, to those who believe in His name: 13 who were born, not of blood, nor of the will of the flesh, nor of the will of man, but of God. NKJV

So if you earnestly prayed to God for forgiveness and salvation, welcome to the family of the living God! There are a few things that you should do right from the start. First, get yourself a Bible and begin reading the Book of John in the New Testament. Next, find a good, Bible-believing church and let them know that you just got saved and need to be baptized. Baptism follows salvation as a public declaration of your new faith. Get plugged into your new church home and begin your new abundant life.

Here are a couple more benefits associated with your new faith in Christ:

Romans 8:1-2
Therefore, there is now no condemnation for those who are in Christ Jesus, 2 because through Christ Jesus the law of the Spirit of life set me free from the law of sin and death. NIV

2 Corinthians 5:17
Therefore, if anyone is in Christ, he is a new creation; the old has gone, the new has come! NIV

If Satan has convinced you that salvation is something that you do not need at this time, you are putting yourself and your eternal destiny in grave danger. Your next breath is not guaranteed. The wrath of God still remains on you because you have chosen to pay for your own sins. There is no other sacrifice made on your behalf for sin other than Jesus Christ.

John 3:18
He who believes in Him is not condemned; but he who does not believe is condemned already, because he has not believed in the name of the only begotten Son of God. NKJV

Romans 2:4-6
4 Or do you show contempt for the riches of his kindness, tolerance and patience, not realizing that God's kindness leads you toward repentance? 5 But because of your stubbornness and your unrepentant heart, you are storing up wrath against yourself for the day of God's wrath, when his righteous judgment will be revealed. 6 God "will give to each person according to what he has done. NIV

Revelation 20:15
And anyone not found written in the Book of Life was cast into the lake of fire.
NKJV

APPENDIX B

*T*here are two very helpful websites that I am recommending to all who have possession of this book. You will find a wealth of information, gospel presentation styles, tools to build your faith, etc. Please take time to visit these websites and see for yourself what a wealth of spiritual knowledge is at your fingertips.

www.livingwaters.com
www.gotquestions.org

May the Lord watch over you and bless you abundantly throughout your Christian journey. In the saving name of Jesus, Amen! Give Him Praise!

CPSIA information can be obtained at www.ICGtesting.com
Printed in the USA
LVOW12s1204180713

343367LV00001B/3/P

9 781626 972018